emotional PURITY

emotional PURITY

AN AFFAIR OF THE HEART

Heather Arnel Paulsen

Foreword by BarlowGirl

CROSSWAY BOOKS

WHEATON, ILLINOIS

The author is represented by the literary agency of The Livingstone Corporation, 351 South Main Place, Suite 110, Carol Stream, Illinois 60188.

This book is produced with the assistance of The Livingstone Corporation (www.livingstonecorp.com). Project staff includes Dana Veerman, Linda Taylor, and Bruce Barton.

Cover design: Jon McGrath

Cover photo: Jimi Allen Photography, Inc.

First printing, 2007

Printed in the United States of America

Library of Congress Cataloging-in-Publication Data

Paulsen, Heather Arnel.

    Emotional purity : an affair of the heart / Heather Arnel Paulsen.

      p. cm.

    ISBN 13: 978-1-58134-855-2 (tpb)

    ISBN 10: 1-58134-855-X

    1. Chastity. 2. Dating (Social customs)—Religious aspects—Christianity. 3. Single people—Conduct of life. 4. Marriage—Religious aspects—Christianity. I. Title.

BV4647.C5P38   2007

241'.66—dc22   2006032418

VP		17	16	15	14	13	12	11	10	09	08
15	14	13	12	11	10	9	8	7	6	5	4	3	2

To Miles and Luke,
you were my inspiration.

Contents

Acknowledgments

TO GOD ALMIGHTY: Words cannot express my deep love and gratitude I have toward You. May You receive all the glory.

To my dear husband, John Patenaude: Thank you for saving your whole heart for me and me alone.

To my faithful parents and sisters, Arne, Julie, Colleen, and Lesli: Without your daily love and honesty this book would not exist.

To the staff at Livingstone: Thank you for your countless hours of editing and pouring yourselves into this project.

Foreword

HERE'S HOW WE MET. On a snowy January weekend in 1999 our family hosted a retreat in Lake Geneva, Wisconsin. The hotel where we stayed was being run by the Paulsen sisters. It was there that we had a chance to met Heather and her family.

Heather was not an author, and we were not BarlowGirl, although we all had the same vision and heart for purity. It is funny how life tends to come full circle! Before any of us knew what God had in store for us, He introduced our families.

Purity

Pursing God's definition of purity has been a passion for us, long before we became a band. We have an intense desire to follow God in the area of physical and emotional purity, and we believe He has called us to bring this message to our generation.

When we were each sixteen, our parents presented us with rings and gave each of us a choice as to whether or not we wanted to really seek God on what true purity really is. To be honest we were already so tired of watching what the whole recreational dating scene was doing to our generation. So we each made a commitment to God and our parents that we would seek out what God's standard of purity was. We would not sell ourselves short and believe the lie that the only path toward marriage is casual, recreational dating.

God showed us that not only did He long for us to remain physically pure, but to save ourselves emotionally as well. Proverbs 4:23 ("Above *all* else guard your heart, for out of it flows the wellspring of life") was the key verse in our journey of giving God our hearts.

Many people think we are crazy when we tell them about our convictions to lay aside recreational dating and pursue Him wholeheartedly during this season of our lives. They do not understand the beauty of saving *everything* for our future spouses! We've met people who think we're pretty off to willingly "miss out" on dating, but our goal is not to be a good girlfriend, it's to be a good wife!

We know that with God we are called to wait on His timing; so we're not thinking about today and what makes us feel happy and accepted now. Our thoughts are with our future husbands, and the joy of being able to give him *all* we have: our first date, our first kiss, our first love, and a complete, whole heart! It belongs to him, and we will wait on God no matter what others think.

This Book

The book you are holding has been an amazing tool in our lives. We are so excited to share this book with you and want to encourage you to open your hearts and minds to a new way of thinking.

The issues that Heather tackles in this book are issues we see everywhere. However, many times they are just swept under the rug or not talked about, until now! Heather has been daring enough to challenge our society's way of thinking about recreational dating and emotional purity!

It's a new way of thinking, but as Christians we are called to "not be conformed to this world, but [to] be transformed by the renewing of our minds" (Romans 12:2). In this book you will see that you cannot receive all God has for you if you conform to the world's standard.

The moment we started reading this book, we couldn't put it down! This book caused us to ask hard questions of ourselves: "Am I treating the single men in my life as brothers, or am I getting my value from 'harmless flirting'?" "Am I sending confusing signals to the opposite sex?" These are just a few of the questions this book caused us to ask ourselves. We pray that as you read this book you will see that God has so much more for you! It's time for us to put aside the things of this world and pursue God with our whole hearts—even if this means doing the things that are not popular!

Thank you, Heather, for being bold enough to write about these very important issues of emotional purity!

Rebecca, Alyssa, and Lauren Barlow
BarlowGirl

Introduction

IT WAS A CRISP, FALL DAY in 1999 when I first sat in front of my computer and began to type a journal to my future children. I always thought it would be interesting to peer into my parents' past through their journal, so I wanted to give my children a window into my world.

I was twenty-four years old, single, and had experienced a handful of relational hurt and pain. I wanted to share what I was (and am) seeing in the world around me—a Christian culture that speaks of abstinence and physical purity but fails to comment on what I believe is a crucial part of close relationships: emotional purity. I am seeing a pattern develop with male/female friendships—emotional closeness with no commitment—a pattern that always leads to heartache and that lays heavy on my heart.

In my own life I have struggled with God's plan for me as a single woman. About three years before I began to write this book, I saw how an intense desire to be married overrode many of my choices. I realized I was always on the hunt for a husband, and this hunt led me to a place of unrealistic expectations and heartache. I knew this wasn't what God wanted to develop in me through my male friendships. I desired to please God in everything, and I wanted Him to take delight in my walk with Him. So I began to search God's Word, and it clearly showed that He desires all my relationships to be pure—beginning with emotional purity.

God also showed me how to have peace. I knew that God would not keep me single a day longer than He planned. Contentment, peace, and joy replaced frustration, worry, and discontent.

As I wrote to my future children, God began to show me that not only was this message for them, but it was also for *all* His children. He began to show me the impact that an understanding of emotional purity could have on the Christian single culture.

After this book was first published in 2001, I traveled and spoke all over the country. I saw firsthand how the message of emotional purity was changing lives. Men and women, old and young, married, single, and divorced—everyone gained a fresh perspective on what God meant when He said, "Above all else, guard your heart" (Prov. 4:23, NIV). It was fascinating to watch God transform His children.

Through the lives of fictional characters, the first chapter provides a reference point for the entire book. Tracy and Mike's relationship represents the male/female interactions between many young Christian singles. Their story helps us begin to unravel the confusing aspects of emotional purity.

The chapters following the story examine their relationship and the importance of guarding your heart. I provide you with tools to remain emotionally whole for your future mate and also share what God's plan is for singles and what God's Word says about emotional purity.

At the end of Chapters 4, 5, 12, and 14 I have included a "For Guys Only" section. Women, I'm sure there are men who you think need to learn a thing or two about emotional purity—these are the "Cliff Notes" for certain sections. These can be read on their own or with the entire chapter. My hope is that young men also will be encouraged to examine emotional purity in their lives.

Although I was single when this book was first published, I did later marry, as shared in Chapter 16 of this new edition. But prior to marriage I did struggle with many of the issues discussed here. I am not sharing theory but real-life challenges and concerns as I and many others have experienced them.

Read with an open heart and mind. I pray that God will speak to you and will use this book in a powerful way in your life. May God bless you as you read.

chapter ONE

Tracy and Mike

SINCE TRACY'S MOVE A WEEK AGO, she had already attended a local Bible church and immediately made a new friend. She felt nervous as she waited for Emma to pick her up for Wednesday night fellowship. As she curled her hair, picked out the right outfit, and fussed over her makeup, her heart said a thousand prayers. Tracy longed for a friend, and having had a great time at lunch on Sunday, she thought maybe Emma would fit the part. The doorbell rang. Six-thirty on the dot.

"Ready?" Emma asked.

Tracy grabbed her jacket. "Let's go!"

It didn't take long to reach the home where the gathering was taking place. Emma rang the bell, but before her finger released the button, the door opened to a tall guy with a welcoming smile. For a moment Tracy felt blown over by the very good-looking man in the doorway. She quickly regained her composure as she remembered that she was not there to meet "the one." He extended his hand toward them. "Hi. My name is Mike Hartman, and you?"

Emma confidently extended her hand. "Emma. Nice to meet you."

"Tracy Kass," Tracy said bashfully and slowly offered her hand to Mike.

Emma continued, "Are you new? I don't recall meeting you before."

"Ye—" Before Mike could finish his answer, a bubbly young girl embraced Emma and swept her into the living room, leaving Tracy alone with Mike.

"So how long have you been attending this group?" Mike motioned for Tracy to enter the house. Without giving her a chance to reply, he kept talking. "Your friend was right—I have never been here before. And can you believe they've got me answering the front door? I met some of these people Sunday at church, and they invited me to this fellowship night. It seemed like a good midweek pick-me-up." Mike stopped to catch his breath. "Sorry, I'm rattling on. What about you? Have you been here before?"

Tracy could not believe how totally comfortable Mike seemed. It made her feel more relaxed in this new environment. "No, this is also my first time attending one of these things. I just moved from Vermont, and I don't know anyone except Emma, and we just met on Sunday."

"Oh, this is cool. Someone new besides me. I just moved from Seattle. I got a job transfer and have only been here a week." He helped her take off her jacket as they walked into the living room together.

"Amazing, I've only been here a week as well." Tracy was surprised that she would meet someone with such a similar experience.

Throughout the evening they found themselves explaining over and over that they were not "together." By the end of the night it became a joke, and Tracy and Mike began acting as though they were together just to fool everyone.

Throughout the evening, Tracy and Mike talked about their moves and the new paths where God was leading each of them. Mike mentioned that he enjoyed tennis, and Tracy was excited to find someone else who liked the sport. Tracy had played on her college varsity team. Both eager to check out the local courts, they planned a tennis match for Saturday afternoon. Tracy could not believe how quickly the hours passed with singing, Bible study, and fellowship. At nearly eleven o'clock, Emma announced that she needed to leave.

Mike opened his arms for a warm hug from Tracy. "I prayed that God would allow me to meet a friend, and I think He answered my prayers." Tracy felt a bit startled by this frank comment, but she accepted his hug.

"See you Saturday," she answered sweetly.

On the way home Tracy beamed with excitement, unable to erase her smile. Emma could see that Tracy and Mike had hit it off. She began firing questions. "Well, what do you think of Mike? You spent the night getting to know him. Is he good-looking or what!"

Tracy hadn't realized the attraction was so obvious. "He is really a nice guy, and we have so much in common. We're going out on Saturday."

"A date already! You go, girl!" Emma said, stunned.

Tracy was a bit taken aback. "I don't think it's a 'date' date. It's just two people going to play tennis."

"Whatever. I could see the way he looked at you. There is definitely something there," Emma replied. "You'd better call me Saturday night and give me the details!"

That night Tracy couldn't sleep for thinking about the friendly people she had met and how awesome the fellowship had been. Her thoughts kept going back to her new friend Mike. Her mind was set—she did not want to be hurt again.

Saturday Tennis

Tracy spent Thursday and Friday evenings on the tennis court, brushing up on her serve. With job hunting and the move she felt out of shape, and she did not want to make a fool of herself on Saturday. Her heart felt warm each time she remembered Mike's engaging embrace.

A good game of tennis was just what Tracy needed after a week at her new job. She felt surprised at how good Mike was. He gave her a run for her money. Afterward they decided to grab a bite to eat.

Tracy felt very relaxed around Mike and wanted to know more about his walk with the Lord. While they munched on burgers and fries she asked, "When did you come to know Christ?"

"Well, I guess I have always known about Him. My parents were awesome examples of Christ, and when I was four I asked Him into my heart. During high school, guys from my Bible study and I started a weekly prayer meeting at school. It's still strong and has seen over two hundred kids come to know Jesus. Another growing experience I had was when I gave up a Thanksgiving at home with my parents to go on a mission trip to Africa." Once started on the subject, Mike seemed eager to keep talking.

"My love for the Lord grew even more in college. My freshman year, I plugged into a Bible study with four other guys. We started a Christian fraternity at my mostly heathen college campus, and it became one of the most respected fraternities. We were referred to on campus as the 'God Squad.'"

Tracy chuckled. Mike went on, "Those buddies have become my closest friends, and we always joke that when we get married our wives will also have to be best friends with each other. Tracy, you'd really like these guys. Okay, enough about me, what about you?"

Tracy saw his depth of character as he shared his deep love for his Savior. Was that comment about his buddies a suggestion that she develop a friendship with his pals? She brought her thoughts back to the conversation and shifted in her seat. "Well, my testimony is not as . . . well, let's just say I have more baggage than you. For starters," Tracy began, "I was not brought up in a Christian environment. We always went to church, but it never meant anything. My folks did the best they could, but in high school I began to rebel against everything and everybody. I . . . well, I walked on the wrong side of the road. As I look back, all I know is that I was trying to fill my heart with something, but God would not allow anything to satisfy me but Him.

"During my junior year of high school I was in a car accident with my boyfriend. We had been drinking, and we hit a tree. Neither of us was injured, but the accident brought me back to the Lord. We broke up, and I started going to church. This time when I went, I was seeking to find the truth, not just going because it was the thing to do. One Sunday the preacher talked about Christ being a part of your every moment, and that is what I wanted. That afternoon my new boyfriend and I accepted Christ. We tried to have a godly relationship, and we were planning to go to the same college, a small Christian college about three hours from my home, but I got accepted and he didn't. We decided that if God wanted us together, then being at different colleges wouldn't matter. But as the summer went on, we felt ourselves being drawn in separate ways. We broke up right before school started.

"At college I had awesome roommates. The three of us prayed

together all the time. They showed me what it means to be forgiven and to forgive myself. I dated a guy in college, and he was another key in my learning to build a deeper relationship with God. We were planning on getting married, but you know how life goes.

"I see God's perfect plan in bringing me out here, so far away from my guy friend. I think I needed to be away from the whole situation. See, he's getting married next spring, and the girl he's marrying is—or should I say was—a good friend of mine. I know that God has my husband picked out for me—I just need to wait on His wonderful timing."

Tracy amazed herself as she released her deepest feelings—and to a man! She went on, "God has used many different people and situations to draw me to Him, and I am thankful that He's a big part of my life."

Tracy glanced down at her watch. "Wow! It's four o'clock." *Where have the hours gone?* she asked herself. She could not believe how much they had shared. She squirmed in her seat and felt it was time to go.

Happy to be home, Tracy swung open the door to her modest apartment. Before the door closed behind her she noticed the red light flashing on her answering machine. She hit the play button before she removed her sweater or dropped her tennis equipment.

"Hi, Tracy. This is Emma. I can hardly wait to hear what happened with you and Mike. It's late in the afternoon—are you still out with him? Give me a call when you get in. I want to hear all the juicy details of your day. I'm so happy for you!"

Tracy didn't lose her smile as she dialed her new friend's number. "Hi, Emma. It's Tracy," she said with a light bounce in her voice.

"Hi, Tracy. I've been waiting for your call. So what happened with your tennis date?"

Not wanting to embellish the day or indulge her friend too much, Tracy simply responded, "It was nice. We did a great deal of talking. He's a great guy, and who knows what will happen?"

Emma fired questions at Tracy: How did he do this? What did he say about that? Tracy wanted to think about the day quietly, so she sweetly said good-bye and headed for the shower. Thinking about Mike brought on a mixture of emotions she had thought were buried after her last breakup. But maybe, Tracy thought, God had brought Mike into her life for a reason.

Friendship Building

One week ran into the next, and before long Mike and Tracy's friendship developed a pattern. Sunday mornings brought them together at worship, followed by an afternoon of lunch and fun with the singles group. Neither missed the weekly Singles Fellowship Night, and then there was the standing date for tennis and lunch on Saturday. Sunday, Wednesday, Saturday. Church, singles fun, tennis. Sunday spiritual bonding, Wednesday social bonding, Saturday fitness bonding.

One night as Tracy wrote in her journal, her thoughts poured out. *Father, You know my innermost thoughts and how much I do not want to have these feelings for Mike, but they are here. He loves You so much, and that quality attracts me to him. He strives to serve You and longs to love You more each day. What should I do with these feelings?* She was thankful that Mike never overstepped physical boundaries; she knew this kept them pure. They were very close, and the closeness was what she valued most in their friendship. As weeks turned into months, Tracy's mind often wondered if this could be the pure relationship she had only dared to dream about secretly.

Friday nights had become one of her few free nights. Tracy used them to tackle life's menial chores. She'd fallen into the habit of picking up her dry cleaning, stopping at the mall or grocery store, then going home to make her weekly call to her family and finally clean up her tiny apartment that she had neglected most of the week. But this particular Friday night her apartment would just have to understand her lack of attention.

On Wednesday night at Singles Fellowship, Emma had made Tracy promise to have a girls' night out. "It's been way too long since we've gotten together," she said. "I feel like we haven't talked in ages." Tracy agreed, and they arranged to meet for dinner and a movie.

Seated in a secluded booth, the pair had just ordered pizza when Emma blurted out, "So tell me, what's going on with you and Mike?" Tracy had felt twinges of eagerness to indulge someone with the happy details of her friendship with Mike. Emma would be a perfect friend to affirm her feelings. Tracy began to talk as the waiter deposited their Cokes, and as they finished the last slices of pizza she was telling Emma of her growing feelings toward Mike.

"Oh, that's normal, Tracy. You two spend so much time together, and he's a nice guy."

"But Mike has never told me his intentions. What if he doesn't like me in that way? I mean, what if he just thinks of me as a good friend?" Tracy asked, hoping for reassurance.

"Tracy, doesn't he text message you a few times a day?"

"Practically."

"Does he hug you hello and good-bye every time you see each other?"

"Yes."

"Does he treat any other girl in the singles group like you?"

"No."

"Doesn't he always give you that playful nudge when you are talking about your tennis matches?"

"Yes."

"Didn't he take you to his coworker's birthday party?"

"Yes—Brice, the guy he led to Christ."

"Didn't he give you a nickname—Squeak or something?"

"Yes, Squeak, like the noise of my shoes when we play tennis."

"Well then, he must like you! All the signs are there."

Tracy's heart skipped. "You think so?"

"Yup." Emma replied.

That was what Tracy wanted to hear. She felt that God was confirming Mike's feelings toward her through their conversation.

The following Saturday's tennis match was a real workout for Tracy. She couldn't keep her mind on the game and ended up chasing balls all around the court. Exhausted and ready for a relaxing lunch, she fell into the cushioned booth and asked Mike to order "anything refreshing" for her. As she sipped on a large iced tea, Tracy began to share with Mike a conversation she'd had with Brice, Mike's coworker, during the week.

"I was shocked when he asked me out. I mean, I hardly know him. We'd just met at his birthday party, but I guess he felt comfortable asking me out. Well, he really isn't my type. I know you just recently led him to the Lord, and I praise God for that, but the last thing I need to deal with is a guy who is new in Christ. I need someone who is solid in the Lord,"

Tracy said with a nervous laugh as she wondered whether Mike was going to pick up the clue that she needed a man like him.

Only then did Tracy realize that she'd been twirling a bit of salad around for several minutes while she chatted. She waited for a look of fear or disappointment in Mike's face at the thought of her dating someone else.

"His question really threw me off guard," Mike said as he dabbed his mouth with a napkin. "Brice asked me if he could ask you out. Now, why would he do that?"

Tracy's head bobbed up from her plate. "He asked you?"

"Yeah, isn't that crazy?" he responded with a partial laugh.

Tracy's mind whirled with uncertainty. *Did they discuss me over a coffee break? Did Mike mention any feelings he has for me to Brice? Mike must have told him it was okay to ask me! What's going on?* She unruffled her thoughts enough to counter, "Yeah, crazy."

"Hey, let's get a movie and go back to my place!" Mike said abruptly as he stood up, grabbed the bill, and paid.

At his home, Mike popped in the DVD and sat down next to Tracy on the couch. At first she was nervous, but then Mike put his arm around her. "Just think, Squeak, if you had gone out with Brice tonight we wouldn't have had such a terrific time."

"This is true," Tracy said as she snuggled effortlessly into his arm. She felt very secure there and briefly reflected that she was thankful Mike was being so cautious with her in regard to physical purity. Tracy couldn't remember a time in many months when she'd had such a complete feeling of protection.

Confusion

Tracy felt homesick and confused. When time allowed, her thoughts would wander back to the stunning fall colors back east. She could only imagine the spectacular show in her parents' well-manicured yard in New England. Envisioning these colors only intensified Tracy's loneliness. Thanksgiving away from her family—their traditional time of baking, taking a gift basket to a needy family, and then the afternoon of feasting and football—threatened to be difficult for her.

Tracy was rather amazed that another little part of her was energized by thoughts of beginning *new* traditions. During one of those reflective moments, Tracy shared her homesickness with Mike by e-mail. She knew he would understand because at one time during high school he had been in Africa over the holidays.

On Saturday Mike asked Tracy what she planned to do for Thanksgiving.

"Nothing, silly. I told you that in my e-mail." Tracy wondered where this conversation was headed.

"Well, I called my folks, and you know what? We have an extra chair at our Thanksgiving table. Would you like to fill it?" Mike asked.

Tracy's heart soared at the thought of meeting Mike's family. At the same time her mind rapid-fired question after question. *Could this mean something? What will I wear? Is there time to lose a few pounds? Will they like me? Will I meet his whole family? Does he want me to meet the folks before he takes our relationship to the next level? He must like me. Are his feelings for me developing?*

The awkward pause of silence forced Tracy back to reality. She blurted out, "Yes, I would love to go!"

Thanksgiving

They made plans to leave a couple days before Thanksgiving because Mike was asked to speak on Wednesday evening for his old high school youth group. The next few days were one big blur for Tracy. Finally the time arrived—the event that had dominated her thoughts for way too long.

As Mike pulled up and quickly placed Tracy's bags in the flatbed of his truck, he gave a brief prayer for safe travel and a holiday to remember. Then off they went.

The next few hours were filled with emotional and spiritual highs. They belted out praise song after praise song, from "Shout to the Lord" to "How Great Is Our God." Tracy felt their spiritual bond grow stronger in those wonderful moments of worship.

Mike gave Tracy the lowdown on his parents and siblings after they discussed Mike's topic for the youth group the next evening. Tracy didn't even notice the remarkable scenery zooming past her window as Mike painted a vivid picture of his family's Christmas. Her full attention was riveted on him as his story led to their mutual promise to exchange Christmas gifts in one month. Tracy's whole world seemed to be contained in the little Toyota truck as they traveled down the road, each hour blending with the last.

Without warning they arrived. As they pulled into the driveway, Tracy glanced at the clock and was stunned. *My how time flies*, she thought.

They left the luggage in the truck as Mike led the way to the house. Any nervousness she felt as the door swung open on this new world immediately melted as she soaked in the warmth of his parents' greetings and hugs.

"We always enjoy getting to know Mike's friends" and "We are so glad you could be with us for Thanksgiving," Audrey and Jack blurted out simultaneously. Tracy was overwhelmed with a sense of kindness and sincerity. Mike and his dad disappeared outside to unload the truck.

Mike's mom gently put her arm around Tracy and led her into the kitchen. Only then did Tracy detect a great aroma. "I hope you like what's for dinner tonight," said Audrey. "I'm glad we have a few minutes to get acquainted before Sara arrives from work and Tommy gets home from school." Tracy smiled, feeling thankful that they'd arrived early enough to allow for some family time that evening.

"Smells great. I can't wait to meet your family," Tracy beamed. "What can I do to help?" Tracy instantly bonded with Mike's mom.

The smell of coffee awoke Tracy the next morning. The house remained silent, so she quietly showered and dressed for the day. Scooping up her Bible, she headed downstairs and anticipated a few quiet moments in the overstuffed corduroy chair she had nestled in the night before. As her foot hit the last step, she spotted Audrey sitting in that very chair. Tracy stopped in her tracks when she noticed a Bible in Audrey's lap, her head bowed. The praying woman's head gently turned as she realized her houseguest was present. She invited Tracy to join her, and that was the beginning of a nearly perfect day. An intimate breakfast with Audrey led to a day of running to the grocery store and then preparing side dishes for Thanksgiving with the women of the family. Dinner was full of pleasant conversation and stories of hilarious, embarrassing family moments.

As Mike and Tracy drove to his youth group engagement, she realized they hadn't been alone since the previous day. Mike was deep in thought, rehearsing his talk. This freed Tracy to enjoy the ride in silence with her own personal reflections. She loved that she could feel so connected to him without speaking a word.

The kids mobbed Mike before entering the church. He looked at Tracy through the crowd and seemed to be saying, "I'm so sorry to leave you stranded alone in a strange place, but . . ." Tracy actually enjoyed hanging out in the background, studying Mike's ease at relating to teens.

After an opening prayer with a round of praise songs, Mike stood before the gym full of adolescents on the verge of adulthood. As Tracy watched him connect with the group of restless teens, she realized that she was falling in love with him. A passion for Christ was all she wanted in a husband, and Mike filled the bill. Tracy tried to focus, but her mind refused to grasp one word of Mike's talk that evening. It chose rather to dwell on a possible future with this man.

The ride home was completely opposite to the ride there. Mike talked about how amazing the night had gone. Tracy sat quietly, allowing Mike to fully unload all of his excitement.

Thanksgiving Day activities intensified Tracy's feelings for Audrey, Jack, Sara, Tommy, and, of course, Mike. She was so engaged in Hartman family activity that she nearly forgot to phone her own family with wishes for a happy Thanksgiving! During the day Tracy occasionally glanced Mike's way with an enormous smile and sparkling eyes. She wanted him to know that this Thanksgiving was more than she could have hoped for.

As Tracy rolled over and rubbed the sleep from her eyes, she jolted into the reality that it was Sunday morning. Only a few more hours until she'd be back in her little apartment. As she lay there in a dreamy state reflecting on the last few days, Tracy realized she was not ready to say good-bye to this family with whom she'd so quickly cultivated a genuine love. She pondered the gentleness of Mike's mom and the carefree attitude of Tommy, who lightheartedly joined his brother in calling her Squeak. Each moment of the holiday held a certain level of importance in her heart. Not wanting to waste one minute of enjoyment with her new friends, Tracy bounded from the covers.

The whole family ate together and lingered over breakfast before heading off to church. Afterward when Mike decided that he and Tracy should get an earlier start back than they had planned, Audrey offered to prepare a sack lunch of turkey sandwiches as the pair packed. As Tracy trudged down the stairs, she felt she was leaving a place she had grown to love.

Tracy hugged each member of the family good-bye. She hugged Audrey tightly, not wanting to let go. Audrey whispered in her ear, "Tracy, you're always welcome here. You're a lovely daughter in Christ, and I know that the Lord has great plans for you." The words brought tears to Tracy's eyes; she could not remember ever hearing such sweet sentiments.

It seemed as if they'd just pulled into the now-familiar driveway and now they were driving away, windows wide-open as they waved until the family was out of sight. Tracy settled into her seat, overcome with a touch of melancholy. As they hit the freeway, Mike verbally began to review the past few days. Tracy's gloom slowly lifted as they laughed at Tommy's fumbled play in the family football game, and the disaster that had ended in rolling-on-the-floor laughter when Sara attempted to play beautician on Tracy's long hair. Mike suggested they break out the lunch as they settled in for the journey.

"You know, Squeak," Mike said, "I don't normally tell people this, but around the holidays I start thinking about having my own family and starting new family traditions. Do you ever desire to start a family and your own traditions?"

"Sure, I do. I can't wait to have my own family," she responded, wondering if he was thinking about establishing those family traditions with her. Their conversation remained on the topic of future goals and the dreams they each harbored. She was comforted by how much they had in common.

As they pulled up to Tracy's place, she said, "This was the first Thanksgiving that the main focus was family and not football. Your family took me in and treated me as a family member. I'm so thankful to you for inviting me."

"I'm glad you were able to come, Squeak. Many times over the weekend I could see the joy that my family brought to you." Mike bent down and gave her a soft peck on the cheek. Their hug lasted a bit longer than usual.

Christmas

For Christmas, Mike gave Tracy a beautiful teal Bible with her initials, T.O.K., engraved in gold on the cover. Their telephone chats, which began as taking only a few minutes to confirm a time and place to meet, evolved into lengthy, soul-searching, late-into-the-night discussions. E-mails traveled back and forth frequently and routinely.

Tracy went home for Christmas. Time away from Mike seemed like eternity. No matter how hard she tried to focus on her family and the gift of God's Son, her mind continually wandered back west and to the previous holiday's memories. Tracy loved to share with her sisters how important her relationship with Mike had become, but this only intensified her feelings of being away from him and made her miss him even more.

After New Year's Tracy had a difficult time containing her emotions and wondered if she could hold them in any longer. Her feelings for Mike had developed vigorously, and she felt reasonably secure that he felt the same. Both agreed to forgo the customary tennis game for just this week to catch up on the sleep they had lost over the holidays, but they planned to meet for a bite to eat and catch up on each other's Christmas news.

Meeting at Tracy's favorite restaurant, she was thankful for the familiar atmosphere. "I'll have the usual," she muttered as she shifted uncontrollably in her seat.

"Do you have something on your mind, Squeak?" he asked. She was struck by his ability to read her like a book.

"Oh no, I'm just tired after the long holiday season," she said. That was not totally truthful, but she was using all her strength not to yell, "I love you!"

Trying to take the focus off her anxiety, Tracy strained to shift the conversation to how she had been able to share Christ's love with her family and how nice it was to be at home. As Mike related stories of his family's Christmas, Tracy's mind and heart raced frequently to the conversation she'd been planning in her mind since Thanksgiving. Lunch ended, and Mike again paid the bill. They parted with a hug, and the long-intended words didn't pass Tracy's lips.

That night she called Emma to relieve some of her frustration. "Hi, this is Emma. I am not home right now, so please leave a message after the beep," the machine intoned. Tracy sighed, then drawled into the phone, "Emma, please call when you get home. I can't hold it in anymore. I'll be up late, so call whenever, okay?"

That week Tracy felt nervous each time she saw Mike. Her heart ached to tell him how she felt, but Emma constantly reassured her that he needed to initiate taking the relationship to the next level.

Change

The following Saturday Tracy ran errands and arrived early at the tennis court, allowing a few moments to sit in the car and collect her thoughts. This was their first tennis match of the new year. She was ready to work off some of the pent-up frustration, growing larger every day, that was keeping her from verbalizing her true feelings to Mike.

Her thoughts rolled into a prayer. *God, please help me today. I need Your strength more every day. You have brought Mike into my life, and it would be an honor to serve You with him. Let Your will be done, and please help me accept it in Your time—which I'd really like to be soon, but I know Your time will be right. Just help me, Lord. I feel so mixed-up.* Her mind whirled out of control. She grabbed her bag and headed inside to exercise away a bit of her anxiety.

She was picking up the key to the indoor court when she heard Mike's familiar voice behind her. "Hey, Squeak, did you get court number 1?" Hearing Mike's voice put a smile on her face. As she answered, she turned to face him. "Yes, I got . . ." Tracy's smile faded fast as she choked and raised her hand to cover her gasping mouth. What she saw did not register in her brain. She felt her face turn pale, and she wanted to run.

Mike stood there holding hands with another woman. Tracy choked again, which helped conceal the tears she felt welling up uncontrollably.

"Squeak, are you all right?" Mike asked as he gently patted her back.

"Yes . . . yes, I'll be fine," she muttered, wishing her Nikes would carry her far, far away—away from this new girl who appeared to be in Mike's life.

"Tracy, I want you to meet my new girlfriend, Chrissy," Mike stated matter-of-factly. "Chrissy, this is Tracy, my great friend, the one I told you so much about. She's been like a sister to me since I moved here," he added as he curled his arm around Tracy's drooped shoulder.

Good friend? Tracy thought. *That's all I am to you? Like a sister? O God, help me!* Tracy looked for a swift way out of this situation.

"Nice to meet you," Tracy stammered, using all the strength she had to be polite.

"Me too. Mike has told me so much about you. I feel like I've known you as long as he has," Chrissy said.

"I thought you two could rotate each round," Mike suggested. "Got the key? Let's go!"

Tracy gracefully excused herself, making her way back to the locker room under the pretense of forgetting her hair scrunchy. "You two get started. I'll be right there." Inside the locker room Tracy found the bench farthest from the door, sat down, and began to weep as shock turned into reality.

What am I going to do? I can't stay in here and cry all day. He doesn't care for me like I do for him. What have I gotten myself into! She splashed her face with cold water. *Lord, help. I need You now more than ever.* Head held high but with lead in the pit of her stomach, Tracy headed for the court with the navy-blue scrunchy around her wrist.

"Hey, Squeak, it's your turn," Mike called as she trotted onto the court. Each swing of the racket represented a blow to her heart. Chrissy sat on the sidelines and watched. Tracy had no competitive spirit. Mike swiftly won each match, which answered Tracy's prayer for a quick end to the pain. Her head pounded with a headache that intensified with each high-five between the flirting pair. She just wanted to be home in her safe apartment, far away from this scene.

Tracy fought back tears while driving and was happy to get home. Falling into her chair, she let the tears overflow, then picked up the phone and called Emma for some comfort.

"Emma, he brought his girlfriend today!"

"What? Wait—who? Mike brought his girlfriend to play tennis? You have got to be kidding!" Emma sounded stunned.

"They were walking hand in hand. He rotated us each round. What was I thinking? He never liked me. See, he started this Bible study at work, and she started coming, and last week she accepted Christ as her Savior. And to top it off he introduced me to her as his 'good friend—like a sister.' I was so humiliated." Tracy became more irritated with each sentence.

Emma tried to help. "Tracy, he led you on! He treated you so different than anyone else in the group. He's such a jerk! You have every right to be mad at him. What are you going to do?"

Tracy thought. "I don't know. I'm sure we won't spend so much time together now that he has a girlfriend—who, by the way, is very perky and cute. I thought I wasn't going to let this happen to me again. We weren't physical at all, and we had such a solid base of friendship. I am just so confused. We were great friends." Tracy pulled the last tissue from the box.

"Let's do lunch tomorrow. Maybe that will help?" Emma suggested.

"I don't think so. I need some time alone. Thanks anyway. You've been a great friend." Tracy hung up the phone and sobbed.

chapter TWO

Avoiding Early Intimacy

TRACY AND MIKE WILL NEVER be as close as they were. How did they fall into the common trap so frequently repeated by singles? In a society where friendships between men and women are common, accepted, and encouraged, why do we have so many broken hearts? Why are emotions spent and hearts bonded, as we saw with Tracy and Mike, with little or no thought that there could be another path?

We must resensitize ourselves to the importance of guarding our hearts from the "just friends" battle wounds that we saw in Tracy. Once these commonly misplaced affections are defined, you will perhaps be better prepared to assess situations that you or others may be experiencing.

Defining Emotional Intimacy

Everyone understands physical intimacy. We call it by many names: petting, making love, having sex, making out—the list is endless. Emotional intimacy is just as important, but what names do we have for it? We have very few, if any, euphemisms for emotional intimacy. Maybe if we know what emotional intimacy is and how valuable it can be, we can begin to give it new names.

How many of us have heard, "Wait until you are married to 'go all the way"'? Chances are, if you have spent any time at church on Sundays, you have heard this biblical command repeatedly. We are told that our bodies are the Lord's temple (1 Cor. 3:16) and that we are not to defile them with fornication (Rom. 13:13), which is illicit sex. This is wonderful biblical truth. When we take the step into marriage, God plans for us to be pure in body (Heb. 13:4). But we will see that God's plan is for us to wait until marriage before "going all the way" emotionally as well.

The *American Heritage Dictionary* defines *emotions* as "agitation of the passions of sensibilities; strong complex feelings." It defines *intimate* as "marked by a close acquaintance or familiarity; very personal or private; a close friend or confidant."

Therefore, emotional intimacy would be a close, private relationship that would invoke strong feelings, passions, and the senses. Most likely you have experienced emotional closeness with other people—a brother or sister, friend, coworker, mate, or parent. But here we are talking about emotional *intimacy*. Think about Tracy and Mike for a moment. How emotionally intimate were they? Their hearts were connected, and they shared a deep bond. They had a strong, private, personal relationship that stirred up deep feelings. Tracy and Mike were emotionally intimate without ever defining that intimacy.

Mixed Messages

Because of this unspoken bond, Tracy was confused about where she fit into Mike's life. Was she his girlfriend or just his friend? Mike never clearly defined his feelings for Tracy, which left her wondering. When the relationship is not clearly defined, you will be left playing the assumption game. When there is no clarity or stated expectation in a guy/girl relationship, someone will be left wondering. This point is critical in understanding the danger of flirting with emotional intimacy before a commitment. It's just as dangerous as flirting with physical intimacy.

Let me explain. I have a few male friends. One in particular has been like a brother to me. Now you may ask how we managed to not step over the line of emotional intimacy. Simple. When I first met Bob we were up front about our feelings. It was clear on both sides that we were just going to be friends. We defined our relationship from the beginning. We treated each other as brother and sister and never expected more than a friendship. Most of the time when we did things together, my sisters, parents, or friends joined us. There was rarely a need for one-on-one time. Over time I came to consider him a true brother. In fact, I had the honor of being a bridesmaid at his wedding, and it felt as though my brother was getting married. I will be honest and admit that he is one of only a handful of guys about whom I have not ever—not even once—wondered, *Could he be the one?* This open honesty was the key in maintaining a brother-sister relationship. We never had to wonder; we never had unmet expectations. It was a beautiful friendship between a guy and a girl.

Contrast that with another male friend I had. We worked together and developed a close friendship. The two of us shared dreams, goals, struggles, and frustrations. We never talked about "us." Not knowing where I stood in his life left me playing the assumption game. My heart ran ahead of my head, and before long I planned our wedding. To my disappointment, our relationship never went past the intimate friendship stage. The pain and hurt I felt caused me to reevaluate the way I handled male friendships.

Although I may have only had one relationship where I was left feeling confused and hurt, my thought life fed my obsessive nature with guys. Here are some real journal entries of mine from ages sixteen to twenty-two:

First guy: I can't stop thinking about him. It's crazy. I don't understand. He is always on my mind. I need help.

Second guy: It was a blast just walking around. We talked the whole time. He is truly one of the greatest guys I know. Through this whole journal it's been about him. I met him on page two and I still can't stop thinking about him. I love thinking about him.

Third guy: He will be at college next fall—who knows what will happen? I could go on and on, but I must stop.

Fourth guy: I really can't get him off my mind. He was here last weekend and we had a ton of fun, like always. I don't know what it is with me falling for my guy friends.

Fifth guy: I really think he is a great guy, but I don't want to feel anything for him. I don't want to like him simply because he is around and gives me attention.

Sixth guy: Father, You know my head and heart are fighting against liking him. It's driving me crazy. My head wants to reject; my heart wants to invest. I feel the need to pull away a little, only because my heart longs for him.

Finally, after years of filling up journals with these types of entries, when God was just starting to teach me what emotional purity looked like I wrote: "So much of my time is consumed by guys. Is that not pathetic? It seems like this is what has ruled my heart—this struggle."

You can clearly see I had OCTD (Obsessive Compulsive Thought Disorder). I used a great deal of my mental energy on guys. Even if you are not sharing deep emotional feelings with a single guy, you can still cross the line with your thought life.

Here's an e-mail I received from a girl who struggled with emotional intimacy:

> I am 21 years old. For three years I have been trying to break free from an emotional affair. When I was 18, my relationship with my youth minister crossed the line and his wife accused us of having an affair. I didn't even know what an emotional affair was, but he kept denying anything so I was left feeling ashamed at my feelings and confusion over whether our relationship was right or wrong. Looking back now, I can see that we did indeed have such an affair. I was in love with this man that was old enough to be my father. Who could I tell? My parents would freak, my pastor would fire him, and my friends would just think I was gross. He went from e-mailing me five times a day to cutting off all communication to win back his wife . . . and I was left with a broken heart.
>
> Time has passed and he and I still talk. Things are back to normal and he is very careful. I know that it is right for him to back off and that what we did was wrong, but my heart still has feelings for him. No matter how much time has passed, I am still in love with him. Not as strong, but it comes in waves. I know that the best way to get over him is to stop all communication, but to be honest I just don't want to lose him. I feel so ashamed. I am still a virgin, yet I feel so dirty. I wake up feeling ashamed, go to bed replaying the movie over and over, and each day I just try to cover the pain with a mask and go on about everyday things. I don't know how to get over it, how to get true freedom.

When a relationship has emotional intimacy without a clear explanation or definition of the friendship, one or both people involved can be left with unnecessary scars. Christian men and women must avoid taking any unnecessary baggage into marriage.

Emotional to Physical Intimacy

Mike Farris stated in an article posted on crosswalk.com (http://www. crosswalk.com/family/parenting/teens/505736.html?page=116083&sp= 1002&p=1015797):

> If a young person starts "falling in love" at 13 or 14 years old, emotional commitments are made and inevitably broken. Pieces of one's heart are given away. After a while, emotional entanglements lead to physical activities. So-called minor activities are first. The activities get more and more intimate as the months and years drag on. After one has been a part of the dating scene for three, four, or five years, the natural physical response to romantic love—sexual intercourse—is tantamount to inevitable.

Did you catch that? Emotional intimacy will bring about physical intimacy.

Emotional intimacy is the kind of closeness and familiarity that stirs feelings and senses that promote a bond, a union that God reserves for the marriage relationship. "Let marriage be held in honor among all" (Heb. 13:4). Once we make a solid commitment and speak the marriage vows, we are free to experience intimacy on all levels: physical, emotional, and spiritual.

That kind of intimacy is also true in the spiritual realm in our relationship with God. When we commit our life to Christ, we are free to have a deep, emotional connection to the pulse and heart of God. It is impossible to have that connection before the commitment.

Hebrews 10:19-22 declares:

> *Therefore, brothers, since we have confidence to enter the holy places by the blood of Jesus, by the new and living way that he opened for us through the curtain, that is, through his flesh, and since we have a great priest over the house of God, let us draw near with a true heart in full assurance of faith, with our hearts sprinkled clean from an evil conscience and our bodies washed with pure water.*

Only after we commit to Christ can we enter with confidence into and enjoy the benefits of a committed relationship with God.

You may be reading this book with a broken past. You may think, *I've messed up time and time again, and I could never be pure again.* Stop right there! God's love and grace for you is bigger than any mistake you have made. He is the healer of past wounds. He longs for you to turn to Him and give Him all your baggage. He wants to change those negative mental tapes you play over and over in your head. Put new messages in your thoughts, and use God's Word as a source for material. Here are some verses to get you started:

If we confess our sins, he is faithful and just to forgive us our sins and to cleanse us from all unrighteousness. (1 John 1:9)

The LORD is slow to anger and abounding in steadfast love, forgiving iniquity and transgression. (Num. 14:18a)

You are a God ready to forgive, gracious and merciful, slow to anger and abounding in steadfast love. (Neh. 9:17b)

The God of all grace, who has called you to his eternal glory in Christ, will himself restore, confirm, strengthen, and establish you. (1 Pet. 5:10b)

God wants to take your heart of stone and make it a heart of flesh (Ezek. 36:26). Only He can take the mess and make something beautiful!

Perhaps you're asking, "How will I ever know who Mr. Right is if I never get to really know anyone?" Or maybe you just can't picture a way out of the intimate friendship you're involved in without hurting the other person enormously. How do you define your current relationship? What is your or your friend's intention with this relationship? Take some time to process these thoughts on emotional intimacy, and in a later chapter we'll go a bit deeper into this multi-layered topic. You may be surprised at the freedom you'll experience when you are guarded from emotional intimacy before its appropriate time.

chapter THREE

Finding Good Guidance

EMOTIONAL PURITY. What comes to your mind when you hear that phrase? Emotional purity is a new concept for most of us, so it takes time to process. May God be a part of this process in a powerful way!

A contributing factor in the lack of understanding of emotional purity has to do with previous generations. In our American culture it seems as though old people hang out with old people, and young people hang out with young people. Generations do not mingle with each other and share ideas, thoughts, wisdom, and feelings. This saddens my heart because there is much we can learn from each other.

Past Generations

Society today is different than it was in the past. Think back a hundred years ago. Young men and women were not allowed to be free in their time together. They were generally chaperoned, and when they spent time together it was for the prospect of marriage. This guidance prevented emotional intimacy and allowed young people to build a strong relationship. As a result, more of them got married. So more people married when emotions were not doled out without some form of commitment. Interesting.

In *Critique of Modern Youth Ministry*, Christopher Schlect examines why as a society we have this idea of "separation of generational influence." Schlect writes, "Grandville Stanley Hall taught that each generation is, or should be, superior to the previous one, and therefore needs to break free from those which precede it." Hall was a pupil of Horace Mann, an evolutionist. Years later we can see how that worldview has played out in all spectrums of life. Most people believe they can gain more insight from their peers than from their old-fashioned parents or grandparents. Sadly, many have bought into this idea that Hall presented—we have looked to our peers, and not our parents, for spiritual growth and emotional guidance.

John Dewey, a student of Hall, is considered to be the father of the modern public school system. Before Dewey, one-room schoolhouses—with children of all ages educated together—were the mode of education. This philosophy that promotes the younger generation as being superior to previous generations flowed right into the modern public school system. With that philosophy so integrated into public education, we can see how easily it has become a part of our thinking and culture. And our Christian society has applied these beliefs. Members of church youth groups and singles groups look to each other exclusively for spiritual growth and fellowship, when they should also be looking to their parents or older members of the body of Christ.

Don't get me wrong. I don't think youth groups and singles Bible studies are wrong in and of themselves. However, I think they present a dangerous breeding ground for youth and singles when these studies are peer-led. Where there is no one older guiding the group, teens and singles are not protecting themselves. Teenagers need older folks, and singles of all ages need guidance as well.

When a woman I know decided to stop attending a singles Bible study, she received a telling comment from a well-meaning friend: "If you don't come to Bible study, how will you grow spiritually?"

In a recent article Erik Johnson says it well:

> Since we were told in the '60s to not "trust anyone over 30" generations have developed a vague distrust of one another. It is a subtle suspicion

that has even infiltrated the church, where it is common for activities to be segregated according to age brackets.

This is unhealthy . . . if we examine biblical attitudes toward the generations, we discover that generational separation is squarely against the tenor of Scripture. ("Joining the Generations," *Discipleship Journal,* July/August 2000)

Mixing Generations

Throughout the Bible we see examples of the mixing of generations. Paul addressed this issue in his letter to Titus (chapter 2), where the apostle said that both older men and older women are to teach and exhort younger men and younger women in different areas. Older men are instructed to teach younger men to be sensible, examples of good deeds, pure in doctrine, dignified, and sound in speech. Younger women are taught to love their husbands, love their children, and be sensible, pure, kind, workers at home, and subject to their husbands so that the Word of God will not be dishonored. Older men and women of the church should teach these godly qualities. Do groups that have peer teachers follow this example?

When people separated themselves by gender, not age, less emotional intimacy took place. Men came calling to a young woman's house not to be friends with her but to look to her as a potential marriage partner. In times past and in other cultures, young people saw the importance of having guidance from their parents and grandparents in this decision. They were not proud in thinking they could do it on their own. And it is obvious that today's methods are not successful.

When we have this free-for-all method, emotions will be hurt and feelings stepped on. Friendship with the opposite sex is a delicate matter and should not be taken lightly. You may be playing with the heart of another person's future spouse.

Emotional purity remains protected when older guidance plays a role in our life. We are thus more protected from falling into an emotional trap. Was Tracy protected from emotional pain? Physically the two were pure, according to our Christian society. However, the line of emotional purity was violated, and Tracy had the pain of another broken heart.

Do you know anyone who has had a similar experience? I'm sure you do. It may be you. I know it has been me. I have allowed myself to become emotionally intimate with men and found myself falling for them. I was hurt when those feelings weren't returned and I heard those words, "Oh, we're just friends!"

I remember watching a PBS show called *American High*. In the show the director asked teenagers to carry around cameras and record their lives as American teenagers. One of the young girls had a "crush" on a boy at school. She said in her video diary that they "just clicked." Two weeks after her confession, he invited her over to his house. When she showed up, another girl was there. She admitted that this broke her heart. She sent him an e-mail explaining her pain. He responded, "You're like a sister to me." She responded back, "Then why didn't you treat me like a sister two weeks ago?" This scenario happens over and over in all races, in all places, and with all ages and types of people.

Recently I received this e-mail from a girl who struggled with her own "Tracy and Mike" scenario.

> Pastor Chris asked me to be a youth leader after I had been saved for about a year. He was known in the congregation as the young, single, and handsome pastor, so I was flattered when he asked me to pray about being a youth leader. I had already considered this option before he approached me, so I know my motives were honorable.
>
> Once I was a leader, I became friends with the other youth leaders, especially Lisa and Rebecca. They were my first group of Christian friends and, being new in my faith, I was eager to have friends who shared my beliefs. We would all go out together after youth group and during the weekend. Chris was always with us.
>
> Lisa and Rebecca contributed in putting the idea of "Chris and me" into my head. I guess they were my "Emma"—like the story in your book. Lisa would tell me that when we were all planning to hang out, Chris would make sure that I was coming. Of course, I started to pick that information apart. "Why did he want to guarantee that I was coming? What could this mean?" In retrospect, he may have just been reaching out to me, a new Christian.
>
> After having hung out for months with my new friends, Chris and I became comfortable with each other. One night, we decided to give each other hand massages. These now-routine hand massages led to us cuddling on the couch. I was surrounded by more mature Christians so it never occurred to me that this was wrong. They would have told

me if I overstepped any boundaries, right? In fact, Lisa and Rebecca told me how cute we were together, how he definitely liked me, and not to worry.

Things didn't seem right. I wanted to be his girlfriend—I didn't want to give away my affection for free. Then, I read your book. My story seemed identical to Tracy and Mike. I told Lisa what I had learned and we agreed we should back off a bit. I'm thankful, through God's grace that I was able to back up and start guarding my heart. One month later, Chris's new girlfriend appeared.

I tried to keep a happy face, but I was hurt and angry. He was a pastor and should have known better. But encouraged by Lisa and Rebecca, I was sure that he liked me even while he was dating his new girlfriend. His relationship ended and we started hanging out as a group again.

Soon, the two of us started hanging out again—dinner, a movie or TV show, and snacks at his house. However, there was always a feeling that this wasn't right. He had made no commitment to me, yet I kept acting as if I was his girlfriend. I finally decided to talk to him. It was probably the hardest thing I had to do. I told him that all that had happened between us confused me. I even told him that I had started to develop feelings for him that went beyond friendship. He apologized and we agreed we would be friends. Things were never the same after that conversation.

He started dating someone else, but I knew her well because a year before she had actually been one of the kids in the youth group! She was now twenty years old and he was thirty-one. You can imagine how some people in the church responded. This caused me to really spiral out of control. I got angry at both of them and went into a tailspin of depression. No one knew it—I'd cry in private and put on a happy face at church. I started to skip church to avoid the new couple and even considered changing churches. I had stopped praying, stopped going to church, dropped out of choir, and didn't hang out with my friends anymore.

It scared me that I let all of this lead me away from God. Every time I did pray, it was about Chris. I was tired of letting this consume me. I was tired of asking God to free me from all of this. I wanted to be beyond it, past the situation. I wanted to get back to God.

I went on a women's retreat with the intention of dealing with this situation. That's when I stopped praying for God to free me of the Chris situation and rather to reveal Himself to me. I stopped praying to be emptied of *him*, and started to pray to be filled with more of *Him*. For me, that was really the turning point—I stopped focusing on Chris and started focusing on God.

I wanted to make sure that I let God shine His light on all of the dark areas of the situation. I had another talk with Chris and I asked him to tell me straightforward that he thought of me as nothing more than a friend. He did, and I felt like that chapter was finally behind me. By asking Chris to be honest with me, it helped keep me from falling back into any illusion that he may have feelings for me. I flung the door of communication wide open, even though I knew it would hurt, in order to avoid more prolonged hurt.

Male/Female Bible Studies

It should not surprise us that older members of the body of Christ are unaware of this problem of early emotional intimacy. When they were in their late teens and early twenties, many of them were already married. Intimate male/female friendships were not freely accepted, and it was understood that when you befriended a person of the opposite sex, it was for the pursuit of marriage.

How different would Tracy and Mike's relationship have been had they gotten to know each other around family or older Christians? How would their situation differ had they both stated their expectations for the relationship up front? Would they have been as prone to share emotions if there were older ears or eyes present? Would Tracy have even spent time with Mike?

At night, when I am tired, my emotional guard comes down and I start saying things I shouldn't. I have been known to share too much with well-meaning male friends, and my endless rambling builds emotional ties that do not belong.

This may sound old-fashioned, but before one-on-one dating was established, many people took a protective approach toward marriage. As a result, the divorce rate was much lower. There is something to be said for some of those "old-fashioned" ideas.

As a result of these cultural changes in relaxed male/female relationships over the past hundred years, the church has filled itself with programs that actually encourage emotional intimacy to take place. But I think it is beginning to backfire. I have seen firsthand how singles and youth groups provide a stage for this emotional free-for-all to take place.

Coed Bible studies are springing up all over. At these studies, men and women are challenged to share deep spiritual issues with one another. This can lead us down a path of staleness with the Lord by taking our focus off Him and placing it on a group or a person in the group. Remember, the devil can appear as an angel of light (2 Cor. 11:14). While it may seem harmless to have these close emotional relationships, that may be a scheme of Satan to pull our focus away from God.

Why do I say this? Men and women who share deep spiritual issues and gain an emotional and spiritual bond with a peer group can become almost married to the group. They cannot seem to go out on a Friday night without a section of the group. They find all they need spiritually and emotionally within that group without a commitment to any one person.

Yes, I do mean "all they need." Once a friend said to me, "Why do I need to get married? I find all I need in this singles group." A closeness develops in these groups, and they can begin to meet not only emotional and spiritual needs but also physical. Making out, heavy petting, and in some cases casual sex is common, tolerated, and almost accepted. There is a promise of accountability in these groups, but I have rarely seen it occur.

Mentors

When I learned to look to my parents, I found freedom to pursue God with all that I am. They had gone through the dating scene themselves and experienced the negative consequences of hurt and heartbreak. Their insight is incredible. The 20/20 perspective I received from my folks gave me a safeguard from repeating generational mistakes.

Solomon repeats this idea a number of times in the book of Proverbs: "Hear, my son, your father's instruction, and forsake not your mother's teaching" (1:8). "My son, be attentive to my words; incline your ear to my sayings" (4:20). "My son, keep my words and treasure up my commandments with you" (7:1). "And now, O sons, listen to me, and be attentive to the words of my mouth" (7:24).

Don't you think we should listen to the wisest man in all history? Solomon knew the importance of having godly paternal guidance, and he also knew that the counsel of the wise is a good thing. Read these other verses about seeking wise counsel:

> *Blessed is the one who finds wisdom,*
> *and the one who gets understanding,*
> *for the gain from her is better than gain from silver*
> *and her profit better than gold. (Prov. 3:13-14)*

> *Without counsel plans fail,*
> *but with many advisers they succeed. (Prov. 15:22)*

Solomon knew that young people needed his advice and the input of other God-fearing people. A great deal of blessing comes from a heart willing to seek guidance from the wise.

And not just blessing—*freedom.* My sensitive heart loves the safety net my parents provide. I know that in the long run I will be thankful I have not spent my time giving emotions to men that they did not rightfully own.

When you experience intimacy without commitment, you are playing with the heart of a fellow brother in Christ, and you will violate emotional purity. With so many singles receiving intimacy—spiritually, emotionally, and physically—from members of the opposite sex, marriage is no longer special. When someone gives away so many pieces along the way, the future husband or wife will not receive the whole heart. Would you feel like a special guest if someone invited you over for dinner and brought out half-eaten, leftover food? "Let's see, your choices are Tuesday's meatloaf, Friday's chicken soup, or three-day-old chop suey."

Emotional purity before marriage allows the greatest opportunity to become emotionally intimate with your mate during marriage. Strive toward emotional purity, and one day you will reap the rewards. God blesses those who desire purity and holiness.

chapter FOUR

Guarding Your Heart

GOD CREATED WOMEN WITH hearts that are more sensitive and emotional than men's. How should a woman's heart be nurtured and protected? Titus 2:4-5 instructs older women to encourage younger women to love their husbands and children. The Greek word for *love* here is *phileo*. Most of the time when you see the word *love* in the Bible, it is the Greek word *agape*. *Agape* means a love that earnestly desires and wants the best for another. *Phileo*, the love a wife is to have for her husband, means friendship, an emotional attachment type of love. This is where we get the name of the city of Philadelphia, the city of "brotherly love."

The Tender Heart

I have yet to meet a woman who, when totally honest with herself, won't admit she has a tender heart. However, after years of being vulnerable and then hurt, many women's hearts have become calloused. When God created Eve, He gave her a tender heart. All of us women have been given the same kind of heart, with the desire to love and be loved. He made women emotional and caring.

Men need to know that women are emotional people; we can become emotionally connected in a matter of moments. Our ability to emotionally bond quickly is heart-glue for our marriage, not for just any male friendship.

This reminds me of a close friend of mine, Connie, who befriended an older Christian man, Joel. Joel flirted with her by tugging on her hair, giving her a nickname, and spending countless hours with her. He was never up front with how he felt, but her heart fell for him, even though she knew she did not want her marriage to begin on such a superficial level. Connie eventually confronted Joel, and he gave the all-familiar brush-off, "Oh, we're just friends." Their relationship took away emotional glue that was meant for Connie's future marriage.

First Love

A woman never forgets her first love. When I spoke at a women's retreat, I decided to test my own theory with a four-question survey about a woman and her first love. The questions were:

(1) Do you remember your first love?

Of the 116 women who participated, 110 answered yes.

(2) Do you still think about your first love?

Of the 116 women, eighty-five replied yes.

(3) Do you have a special place in your heart for your first love?

Nearly half answered yes.
The final question made the room gasp:

(4) Did you marry your first love?

Only seventeen of those 116 women married their first love!

After the confession that their first love did indeed still have a special place in their hearts, many had to say that they did not marry their first love.

I concluded that a woman never forgets her first love. Actually many older women can still tell you specific details about their first love—first date, first kiss, etc. My mom and dad went to a Valentine's party a few years back. They watched a *Newlywed*-type of game with people married forty-plus years. When the men were asked what their wives wore on their first date, most of them made it up. The women, however, remembered *everything*, right down to the bobby socks and poodle skirts. Not only did the women remember the event—they also remembered the details surrounding that emotional attachment. The men's eyes twinkled as they heard their wives describe that special time when they both experienced the emotional rush of infatuation.

Understanding the Differences

God created women with different emotional needs than men. If we were created alike, then God's commands to us would be identical. Notice how they are written (emphasis is mine):

> *Likewise,* husbands, *live with your wives in an understanding way.* (1 Pet. 3:7)

> Husbands, *love* [agape] *your wives, as Christ loved the church.* (Eph. 5:25)

> *Older* women . . . *train the young women to love [phileo] their husbands.* (Titus 2: 3-4)

> Wives, *submit to your husbands, as is fitting in the Lord.* (Col. 3:18)

Men's inspired command is to love their wives and to be understanding with them so as not to hinder their own prayers (1 Pet. 3:7). Women need to learn to be subject to their husbands and to let "the hidden person of the heart with the imperishable beauty of a gentle and quiet spirit" (1 Pet. 3:4) guide their words, thoughts, and actions.

Since we are created to be different, single men and women need to take responsibility for how the other person will react to the attention each is giving. We don't want to cause a fellow brother or sister in Christ to stumble, stray, or lose his or her focus on God.

What if Mike had been aware that creating an environment for Tracy to share so openly caused her to be more focused on their friendship than on her relationship with God? Would he have been more cautious?

If he had seen Tracy as a potential marriage partner, how would he have treated her differently? If Tracy had not been emotionally open to Mike, it's possible she would have appeared to be a little prudish. Emma might have prodded her with questions such as "What's so wrong with spending time with him?" or "You guys seem to click, why not just jump in blindfolded with both feet? You know the old saying, 'It's better to have loved and lost than never to have loved at all.'" I know people who thought I had fallen off my rocker because I chose to not be emotionally available to just any guy who came along. How sad that we look at the ways of the past and think of them as outdated when in reality our modern ways of thinking have opened the door to all kinds of hurts. I have been teased because of my desire to remain emotionally pure. I have been called a Puritan and peculiar. Well, what's so wrong with being called either of those? Christians should strive to attain purity in all areas of life.

Stealing Hearts

We not only give our hearts away—sometimes we actually *steal* the hearts of the men around us. How do we do that? Through defrauding each other. Defrauding sounds like a courtroom term, but it is often what we do to our brothers in Christ. What is defrauding, and how can we avoid defrauding others?

Enhanced Strong's Lexicon states that the word *defraud* comes from the Greek word *pleonekteo* (pleh-on-ek-teh´-o), which means "to have more" or "to gain or take advantage of another, to overreach." *Pleonekteo* is derived from the Greek word *pleonektes* (pleh-on-ek´-tace), which means "one eager to have more, especially what belongs to others."

Webster defines *defraud* as "to swindle or cheat."

What does defrauding have to do with being friends? Basically you defraud people when you use them or cheat them of something they need to save for someone else. One could define it as teasing them with what they cannot have. When you play with the emotions or expectations of someone without expecting to satisfy them in a righteous way, you are defrauding him or her. You cannot righteously satisfy another person until you make a commitment.

The Word clearly tells us to not defraud one another. First Thessalonians 4:3-6 (NASB) states:

For this is the will of God, your sanctification; that is, that you abstain from sexual immorality; that each of you know how to possess his own vessel in sanctification and honor, not in lustful passion, like the Gentiles who do not know God; and that no man transgress and defraud his brother in the matter because the Lord is the avenger in all these things, just as we also told you before and solemnly warned you.

This passage continues the thought of sexual immorality and lustful passions by warning us to not "defraud" a brother in this matter. Why? "For God has not called us for the purpose of impurity, but in sanctification" (v. 7, NASB), or "For God did not call us to be impure, but to live a holy life" (NIV). "So, he who rejects this is not rejecting man but the God who gives His Holy Spirit to you" (v. 8, NASB).

In a dialogue between Jesus and the rich young man, Jesus told him, "Do not defraud" (Mark 10:19).

In our society there is a common acceptance of defrauding one another in uncommitted, emotionally intimate friendships between men and women. We have become desensitized to the emotional purity of our friends. We defraud each other in this arena without even realizing what we are doing.

As we saw in the Greek, *defraud* derives from a word that means taking something that is not yours. What did Mike take from Tracy that was not his? He took parts of her heart and emotions. What did Tracy take from Mike? She took the time and energy he should have been using to serve the Lord and grow in his relationship with his Maker. Both of them took something that did not belong to them; they emotionally defrauded each other.

Tracy and Mike were connected emotionally and spiritually. They passed the point of no return. Tracy allowed herself to become attached to Mike with no solid evidence of his intentions. Once she became emotionally and spiritually involved with him, there was no way for her to leave the friendship without some bumps and bruises on her heart. "Above all else, guard your heart, for it is the wellspring of life" (Prov. 4:23, NIV).

How does defrauding occur during a simple dating relationship? Maybe this familiar example will shed some light on what I mean.

A guy and a girl begin to date each other. They are in the stage of getting to know each other, so they spend a great deal of time together.

Physical activity never reaches the point of intercourse, but they visit the edge once or twice. They spend the holidays with each other's families; they pray together about their relationship, but all along there is no talk of marriage. They have a very "normal" dating relationship. After spending a year getting to know each other with no commitment to the future, the guy realizes she is "the one" and decides to pop the question. She is overwhelmed with apprehension, says she's not ready to be committed, and decides to "take a break from the relationship." They never do get back together, and the guy has a broken heart, wondering if he will ever become that close to anyone again.

How did they defraud each other? Take a closer look at their relationship. They had emotional, spiritual, and physical intimacy without a solid commitment to protect them from the start. They had this intimacy with no long-term commitment—they defrauded each other. They took time, energy, and emotions from each other. They took parts of each other's hearts that did not belong to them.

Sanctification

Let's go back to 1 Thessalonians 4:6, where Paul states, ". . . that no one transgress and wrong his brother in this matter, because the Lord is an avenger in all these things." The NIV says it this way: "In this matter no one should wrong his brother or take advantage of him." The "matter" Paul is referring to is explained in verses 3-5: "For this is the will of God, your sanctification; that is, that you abstain from sexual immorality; that each of you know how to possess his own vessel in sanctification and honor, not in lustful passion, like the Gentiles who do not know God" (NASB).

We see in verse 4 that God calls us to "sanctification" and "honor." Sanctification is the act of purifying yourself, holding your "vessel" or body in honor, respecting yourself. When you cross lines into deep emotional and spiritual connections, you take pieces of another's emotional and spiritual purity that need to be saved for that person's marriage partner. And when you give your heart away, you are giving what belongs to your future mate. Will you be able to present your whole heart at the wedding altar, or have you left pieces of your heart with others? Christ came so that we may be presented before God as holy and blameless, beyond reproach. We, the church (His bride), are to strive toward all purity so that we may be presented before Christ (our bridegroom) holy and blameless. We should reflect that in our earthly marriages.

Let's say you just bought a shiny new convertible Mustang with all the extras. After leaving the lot you run some errands. When you are done shopping, you come out to your car to discover that the 1985 Buick next to you put a dent in your door. Not a large dent, just enough to scrape off some of the paint. If this happens too many times, it affects the value of the car. It is the same way with the human heart. When a heart goes through nicks, bumps, scratches, and bruises, it loses the newness for the correct owner.

The Future

A single person needs to consider that he or she may be dealing with another person's future husband or wife. Would you like to know that your future husband is right now giving himself emotionally and spiritually to another? I would venture to say that none of us would like that too much. If Mike marries his new girlfriend, what about the connection he had with Tracy? His wife will always know about the deep bond they shared. All this could have been easily avoided had Mike not pursued a close friendship with Tracy unless he was very clear with his intentions.

Mike did not completely understand what Tracy was going through, nor should he have. Maybe he had a clue of what she was feeling, but really he was enjoying the stroking of his male ego. After all, Tracy was beautiful and gave him attention. Tracy also gained selfish pleasures from the relationship, being cared for and feeling protected. Because they walked this fine line of emotional free-for-all, Mike's "out" was simply to say, "I just don't understand women." I agree totally. However, he's not required to understand *women* but *one woman*. Remember the Bible says, "Husbands, live with your wives in an understanding way" (1 Pet. 3:7). Peter's not saying, "Live with *women* in an understanding way!"

Learning about the heart of a woman could take a lifetime. God created male and female to represent His whole being. He is the God of understanding and can open our eyes to purity in all areas.

For Guys Only

The female heart is a mystery to most men. One guy who read this book said that he was thrilled to learn about the female heart in one short chapter. I don't think someone can fully explain the heart of a woman in one chapter, but I do hope to help you guys understand how women think.

Emotionally Connected

Women are emotional. I'm sure most of you aren't too shocked to hear that statement. You've watched us cry at movies and turn every friendship into an emotional drama. Women are emotional in all their relationships and can become emotionally connected in a matter of moments.

A woman's ability to emotionally connect quickly is heart-glue for her marriage, but not for all of her male friendships. Think of this: Your future wife, if she remains emotionally whole, will have all of her heart to give to you and to you alone. This should be an exciting thought because you know your wife will experience things emotionally, physically, and spiritually with you and no one else.

Women aren't the only ones who can be emotional. Men need to be just as careful about emotional purity. The norm is for men to be more physically charged. However, I know some men can become emotionally attached easily. I have received e-mails from wounded men. I remember one particular e-mail from a man who felt a strong connection with a female "friend." He and I corresponded for a bit, and I challenged him to DTR (define the relationship) with his friend. Unfortunately, he ended up heartbroken when she did not reciprocate the feelings he had for her. But at least he found out her true feelings before he invested any more of his heart.

Emotionally Charged

Women tend to become emotionally charged in totally different ways than men. For example, if you are paying special attention to a young lady and you have no intention of taking this friendship to the next level, you are emotionally charging her up. She is planning your wedding, naming your kids, and planning your family vacations. This is how most women think.

Men are more physically charged. It doesn't take much for them to long for physical intimacy. Women generally need emotional connection before there can be a physical connection. Our need for emotional connection is as strong as a man's need for physical connection. God created us this way, and He asks us to wait to experience both.

Capturing a Girl's Heart

Knowing that the things you do can emotionally charge a woman, it is important to be very careful how you treat the women in your life. Do your actions convey how you really feel about her and your relationship? Are you leading her on—capturing her heart, with no intentions?

Capturing a girl's heart, attention, and loyalty before a man knows how he feels about her can be compared to his stealing a hot rod to take a joyride. Would he risk being caught with a stolen car, then having to pay the consequences, all for a momentary cheap thrill? Those pride-filled seconds in time, which may have been full of excitement and adventure, may reap a lifetime of paying the price. This is exactly what happens when you toy with a woman's emotions without commitment. The joyride may be an emotionally satisfying, ego-stroking, and self-pleasing experience, but it could hurt both of you.

The female heart should be protected. Ask yourself what you can do to help the women in your life protect and save their hearts for their mates.

chapter FIVE

Defining a Friendship

CAN A MAN AND A WOMAN BE "just friends"? How does friendship play out in dating, courtship, and marriage with a biblical perspective? God created husband/wife relationships here on earth to help us see more of His love. Marriage should be a taste of heaven. Allowing God to show us healthy boundaries in relationships is a key to maintaining emotional purity.

No Obligation

All too often Christian men and women emotionally defraud each other by asking for feelings with no obligation. They toy with commitment-free relationships. We need to be careful. As women we can defraud men by the clothes we wear. Provocative clothes can steal the heart of a man. Men should learn to avoid the Proverbs 7 woman about whom Solomon warns young men, "Let not your heart turn aside to her ways; do not stray into her paths, for many a victim has she laid low" (vv. 25-26a). When a woman dresses in a way that steers a young man's heart her way, she may whet an appetite she has no business whetting.

We all can understand the beauty of saving our physical bodies for our mates. How much more wonderful if we save our emotions as well.

When one avoids defrauding, blessings will follow. I try to spend little one-on-one time with any guy. I am not emotionally available to every young man who comes my direction. I have not held a guy's hand in years or had a deep emotional or spiritual conversation with a male "friend." Now let's imagine that I remain physically pure for my husband but hold hands with other guys, spend one-on-one time with them, and have deep emotional connections with good guy friends. What does that take away from my husband? My appreciation. Do you know how thankful I will be when I am able to share those common things with my spouse? Very thankful! I will praise God for allowing me to be alone with him, hold his hand, share all of my heart with him, and have his arms around me. All these experiences will be new to me. It will be an adventure to share it only with the man I will be married to for the rest of my life—could it get any better? Finding and maintaining emotional purity before marriage will greatly enhance your marriage—that is true romance!

Reexamine Tracy and Mike's friendship, applying this knowledge of commitment first, then emotional intimacy. If Tracy and Mike had been more careful with handing out emotions, there would have been a completely different outcome. Tracy guessed, wondered, and imagined what Mike thought about their relationship. A friendship becomes dangerous at this point. Having no idea what a friend thinks creates a vacuum for you to fill with your own ideas and goals for the friendship.

I know this concept is weird, and I have had to rethink many of my own male friendships. The world's view does not help. The other day I was listening to a Christian radio program about dating and physical purity before marriage. The young man talking hit the target about physical purity. Then he said, "A single person needs to have lots of male/female relationships in order to know how to relate to the opposite sex." I disagree. When we view our relationships through the model of Christ and the church, we see no intimate friendship stage. Once we experience intimacy with the Lord, we have already made a lifelong commitment. We are not allowed to be intimate with Him without that commitment.

Do I think it is wrong to have male/female friendships? Of course not! I have a few as well. However, the danger is the emotional free-for-all that Christian singles play around with in their relationships. Emotions are given, tossed about, and sometimes stolen without a cost.

Susan Nikaido put it well recently in *New Man Magazine*: "If a man *tells* a woman he just wants to 'be friends' but he *treats* her like it's more than a friendship, she will believe his behavior instead of his words" (this is quoted on www.sfcnyc.org/forums/index.php?s=aa36233eaa18fd89b155bd459c9c c5f3&showtopic=2696&st=0&#entry6052). With the free-for-all we have, this scenario happens over and over in the Christian singles circle.

A Defined Relationship

My guy friends and I define our relationships. There is no wondering if one of them is "the one." With these boundaries, we are free to enjoy each other's fellowship as brothers and sisters in the Lord.

I have also met some "marriageable" men, and we have not had this "Where do we stand?" conversation. But because I have set my boundaries and know full well that God is in control, I treat these men the same way I would anyone. As our relationships stand, they will one day be other women's husbands. I do not pay special attention to them, and I keep my thoughts captive to Jesus Christ. I have to control my actions and thoughts because there is no commitment or expectation of a lifelong partnership with any one of them. This takes work, my friend, but in the end everyone will be better off.

Understand that even with these friendships, there is still a level of emotional ties because with any friend there is some connection or we wouldn't be friends. The brother/sister relationship is an excellent guide for me in these friendships. When there is no commitment or hope of a long-term future with a man, the emotions stay in their proper place, not focused on the what ifs but on the now. You can have this type of relationship without the defining-the-relationship conversation. This will take self-control, many prayers, and a few reality checks, but it will save heart pain in the end. As in actual brother/sister relationships, there is never any guesswork about the relationship.

When I spend time with my male friends I ask myself three questions:

(1) Would I be treating him this way if his wife were here?
(2) Would I be thinking about him if I were married?
(3) Would I be saying this if my husband were here?

Answering these questions has helped me maintain emotional purity.

Understanding

For men and women the dilemma of understanding each other is centuries old. It seems one gender is always trying to understand the other but to no avail. So much confusion still occurs. I am no expert on men, but having grown up in a family with two older sisters, I would say I'm an expert on women. The three of us have spent hours searching our own hearts and closely examining all the weird things we do.

Tracy would have fit perfectly into our household. She is emotional, sensitive, and has a fragile female heart. Tracy mentally envisioned herself married to Mike, fitting right into his family, experiencing the protection of a strong spiritual leader, and enjoying a close friendship-leading-to-marriage relationship. In reality they were just friends—nothing more, nothing less.

We aren't really sure how Mike viewed Tracy, but he enjoyed his newfound friend and did not give much thought to his future with her. Chances are, he saw this as a perfectly normal, healthy, twenty-first-century, godly friendship.

Actually, as you read the story most of you probably saw this as a normal friendship between a brother and sister in Christ. Tracy and Mike enjoyed each other's company while remaining physically pure. But something went wrong. This friendship took a wrong turn.

Keep in mind that God created marriage to be an example of the relationship between Christ, the Bridegroom, and the church, His bride (Eph. 5:23-32; Rev. 19:7-9; 21:2). God wants the relationship between a husband and wife to mirror the relationship between Christ and the church. Since marriage begins at the commitment level, we need to line up friendship, dating, courtship, engagement, and marriage with God's depiction. Why should our path toward earthly marriage look or act differently? Our path should be commitment and *then* intimacy.

For Guys Only

How does friendship play out with men and women? What does emotional purity mean in your friendships with women? It is important to understand how a woman thinks and how your actions or words can cause her to think more of your relationship than you do.

What You Say

Take a careful look at your female friendships. Are you telling one of the women in your life things you wouldn't tell most people? She'll notice. She'll see how you share your heart with her. Most girls find this very attractive. When you have a deep and emotional conversation with a girl, you could be stirring her affection and heart toward you.

A man's tender attention and smooth words can steal a girl's heart. However, the young girl in the Song of Solomon requests repeatedly not to arouse or awaken her love until she pleases (2:7; 3:5; 8:4). Men, when you treat a young lady as "special," you may be whetting her appetite for marriage.

This does not mean you have to stop talking to women altogether, but it does mean that you need to be aware of what you say. Talk to all girls equally. The more you share with a young lady, the more you may be causing her to draw closer to you.

How You Act

Guys, this is a big one. Even more than what you say, your actions affect her feelings toward you. A woman believes actions more than words. Girls pick up on everything, and we overanalyze every little thing you guys do.

For example, if you ask a girl to wrap your Christmas presents, she thinks, *Oh, he wants a reason to talk about me at Christmas.* (This really happened to me, and that's really what I thought.) Or if you happen to run into her at the store and ask her to help you shop, she thinks, *He needs me, he really needs me.* Even something as little as where you sit in church may cause her to overanalyze. She may think, *He's sitting there so he can see me.*

That sounds crazy for sure, but that's how women are wired. I remember countless times I'd scrutinize the silliest little thing. One example that comes to my mind is a crush I had in college. I knew the guy's class schedule; so I knew what building he'd be in, on what days, and at what time. I'd *happen* to be there when he'd get out of class. If he'd stop and talk I would think, *There's hope—he must like me.* If he just waved and walked past I would think, *Oh no, what did I say? What did I do yesterday?*

However, understand that the way a girl reacts to how you treat her is not all your responsibility. She must look at how you treat all girls. This is why if you are not interested in a young lady, you must treat her the same way you treat all your other friends—male and female.

A friend of mine is very outgoing and friendly to people. If Joe is at a party, it's a *party*. He knows how to include everyone, and he has a way of making anyone feel special. That's just Joe. A young lady who doesn't know Joe might think, *This guy is super-friendly, and he called me to invite me to a social gathering.* But as she gets to know him, she needs to realize that he not only called her but twenty other people as well. I remember telling Joe to make sure he treats everyone the same. That way if a girl is reading into his actions, *she* is the one at fault, not him.

Being Aware

I think friendships between men and women can be a great learning experience, satisfying and fun. I am not against friendship. I ask you guys, however, to just be aware. Realize that most women you come in contact with are someone else's future wives. Help your sisters in Christ save their devotion for their future husbands. This awareness will be a blessing to her, to you, and to your future mate.

chapter SIX

Protecting Your Relationships

WHAT IS AT THE HEART OF emotional purity before a commitment? Think about areas of your life where you make commitments. When you obtain a mortgage, you make a payback commitment before the bank lends you the money. Your commitment protects the bank. When you join a fitness club, you make a commitment to pay the dues. Your commitment protects the club. Life comes with commitments. In order to enjoy a house, a new car, or a satisfying workout, you have to make a commitment.

Have you ever worked on a group project in which one member of the group did the bare minimum? What a frustrating situation. It's like pulling teeth to get this member to complete his or her fair share of the project. Then when you turn in the project, the slacker receives the same grade as those who worked diligently. The slacker receives the benefits of the grade but never made a commitment to the project. Just like the project slacker, the relationship slacker will seemingly benefit at the expense of others.

Intimate Friends

Many of you would say that friendship is important in marriage, and I would wholeheartedly agree, but are you an intimate friend with Christ before you make a commitment? No! You grow into a deeply intimate friendship with Christ after you make a commitment. Why do we allow ourselves to think that God would be pleased with dating, friendships, courtships, or marriages here on earth that look different than His design for our walk with Him? God does not play games. He does not tease you with emotional highs and lows to draw you to Him. He does not befriend you only to leave you at an emotional low while He goes on to the next emotional high with another friend. He asks for a solid commitment and does not take a halfhearted vow.

Guy/girl platonic relationships need to be reexamined. We must scrutinize what we are doing and see if it fits into God's plan for friendship and marriage. Many singles walk around with battle scars—emotional wounds created by undefined intimate friendships. There is a proper place for platonic relationships, and we must find that place in order to guard our hearts.

Joshua Harris examined male/female friendships in his book *I Kissed Dating Goodbye*:

> Being just friends with members of the opposite sex doesn't just happen by accident. We have to fight for and guard our friendships. Like magnets, men and women are designed to attract each other. But until we're ready to be "stuck for life," we need to avoid premature intimacy.

With God's plan for dating, courtship, engagement, and marriage, we need to take a step back and look at the big picture. Have you ever had the chance to visit the Rocky Mountains? They are spectacular. They go on for miles and miles. I had the opportunity to live in Denver for a year, and I developed a deep love for the mountains. Throughout the year I saw the mountains from many different perspectives. When you take the cog railway up to the top of Pike's Peak, along the way you see only rocks and boulders—you don't see the full view of the mountains. But when you reach the top, the sight is breathtaking—you can see for hundreds of miles. From the top, the picture of the Rocky Mountains is grander than the view on the ride up. Let's not focus on the rocks without looking at the bigger picture. God's ways are always better than what we could do for ourselves. They may require more patience, but in the long run they prove to be amazing!

Friendship Base

When God gave Moses the blueprint for the Tabernacle, He created a room where only the high priest would meet Him, the Most Holy Place. The high priest could enter this room only once a year, and he could only do so because of the shed blood of an animal sacrifice that atoned for his sins and the sins of his people (Heb. 9:1-7). A thick veil separated the room from the rest of the Tabernacle. This was a place of supreme intimacy with the Father (Exod. 25:22). Now because of Christ's shed blood on our behalf, we are invited into this place of intimacy.

> *Therefore, brothers, since we have confidence to enter the holy places by the blood of Jesus, by the new and living way that he opened for us through the curtain, that is, through his flesh . . . let us draw near with a true heart in full assurance of faith, with our hearts sprinkled clean from an evil conscience and our bodies washed with pure water. (Heb. 10:19-20, 22).*

The author of Hebrews is talking to his brothers and sisters in the Lord. To enter into that family, we must accept Jesus as personal Lord and Savior. Only *after* we enter into a lifelong commitment with God may we come into the Most Holy Place of intimacy with Him. *Step one:* a lifelong commitment. *Step two:* intimacy. It is impossible to love Him before step one, and He does not let us get to know Him personally before the commitment.

The no-intimate-relationship-without-a-commitment lifestyle may not be the easiest road to travel. God's ways are difficult, and at times it may feel as though we are swimming upstream. His ways always have long-term benefits; unfortunately, we have a tendency to gravitate to the short-term pleasures of the moment. God desires for us to be obedient, and then the blessings follow. Obedience to Him expresses our love for Him. Philippians 2:8-11 says:

> *And being found in human form, he humbled himself by becoming obedient to the point of death, even death on a cross. Therefore God has highly exalted him and bestowed on him the name that is above every name, so that at the name of Jesus every knee should bow, in heaven and on earth and under the earth, and every tongue confess that Jesus Christ is Lord, to the glory of God the Father.*

We must follow Christ's example of obedience. Let's be more aware of emotional and spiritual purity with others and choose wisely those with whom we share our hearts, emotions, and minds. Our hearts are to be guarded at all costs. God will bless those who seek Him with a pure heart. He wants us to love Him with our heart, soul, mind, and strength.

First Commitment, Then Intimacy

Without a solid commitment in a relationship, the walls around the heart are not protected. Commitment equals protection. When a man and a woman become emotionally and spiritually intimate without commitment, one of two things will happen: They will marry or they will break up. God the Protector says, "Guard your heart, for it is the wellspring of life" (Prov. 4:23, NIV). There is a role here that we must play to avoid being hurt by emotional and spiritual intimacies outside of God's will. God's Word tells us to protect our hearts. Guarding your heart will require you to discern when to share and when to hold back. Pray that God will give you wisdom and will sensitize you in ways that protect your heart.

Broken hearts do not mend easily. With every emotional tie that is damaged by an emotional breakup, little pieces of the heart are lost. If this happens too often, a person can have permanent emotional damage. The more broken pieces, the more difficult is a future spouse's repair. Our goal is to give our mates whole hearts that can become emotionally intimate quickly.

Protecting your heart is not an easy task, but it is essential if the goal—to save all of your heart for your future mate—is to be fulfilled. For some of you, protecting your heart may require less flirting; for others, it may require not giving special attention to a friend.

For a friend of mine, sheltering her heart looked something like this: She received a pleasant e-mail from a guy friend. He said she was beautiful and told her how her new haircut added to her beauty. He went on to say he'd like to write to her and nonchalantly added that he was "single again." What would you make of this letter? My friend knew this guy was not God's choice for her; so she let him know that what he'd said was way outside the bounds of their friendship. She informed him that their relationship would never lead to marriage. He responded with an angry e-mail, accusing her of being the one who was out of line because he'd never mentioned matrimony.

What was he doing? He was asking, in a back-door manner, for her heart with no commitment. When she confronted him, he characteristically shifted blame to her. This story is reminiscent of the Adam and Eve syndrome: "The man said, 'The woman whom you gave to be with me, she gave me fruit of the tree, and I ate'" (Gen. 3:12).

If Christian singles made a pledge not to pursue a deeply intimate relationship with another person without the explicit intent of taking the relationship to marriage, I believe there would be more people married and fewer divorces in the Christian culture.

The *need* for a marriage partner is gone when emotions are *freely* bestowed on anyone who comes along. I hope my future husband will be starving for female attention. If other girlfriends have filled in my place, my husband won't be longing for me. But if he waits until God introduces us, he will be lonely for female attention and companionship and will appreciate me a great deal more.

God is the God of a protective covenant. The commitment you make to God when you choose to accept the gift of salvation allows complete, open, and honest communion with Him. When someone has had a string of boyfriends who let her down, how will she fully trust that it won't happen again? God can heal many hurt hearts. Learn to trust God with your emotions. He longs to protect you with His healthy boundaries.

chapter SEVEN

Learning True Contentment

HAVE YOU EVER BEEN ENVIOUS of someone else's job, house, money, or marriage? I have. When we don't obtain what *we* think we deserve, the envy monster may rear his ugly head. He tells us that we *do* deserve it and that we have the right to pout about not receiving our heart's every whim.

When we allow envy to creep into our lives we allow the envy monster, Satan, to have his way. One pitfall that singles must avoid is envying those who are married.

At one point when was I struggling with being single I heard a preacher say, "To be envious is to doubt God's love for you and His sovereignty in your life." Wow! That hit home for me. I did not trust God's love for me. I believed the lie that married people were more special to God than me, a single person. Just because you are single does not mean God loves you any less than He loves your married friends. God loves you the same. This is a common lie that Satan loves to throw our way to take our focus and trust off the Father.

Throughout the Bible, envy and covetousness are on the lists of behaviors of the ungodly and those who will not inherit the kingdom (emphasis is mine):

You shall not covet your neighbor's house; you shall not covet your neighbor's wife, or his male servant, or his female servant, or his ox, or his donkey, or anything that is your neighbor's. (Exod. 20:17)

For you may be sure of this, that everyone who is sexually immoral or impure, or who is covetous (that is, an idolater), has no inheritance in the kingdom of Christ and God. (Eph. 5:5)

For we also once were foolish ourselves, disobedient, deceived, enslaved to various lusts and pleasures, spending our life in malice and envy, hateful, hating one another. (Titus 3:3, NASB)

Therefore, putting aside all malice and all deceit and hypocrisy and envy and all slander, like newborn babies, long for the pure milk of the word, so that by it you may grow in respect to salvation. (1 Pet. 2:1-2, NASB)

God desires us to be content with the path He has marked out for us.

The Key to Contentment

A key to having a deep personal relationship with God is contentment. Why? Easy. When you are fully content, you say that you are 100 percent totally willing to accept whatever God wants to throw your way—the good, the bad, and the ugly. Look at Jesus' heart of contentment toward the Father:

Have this mind among yourselves, which is yours in Christ Jesus, who, though, he was in the form of God, did not count equality with God a thing to be grasped, but made himself nothing, taking the form of a servant, being born in the likeness of men. And being found in human form, he humbled himself by becoming obedient to the point of death, even death on a cross. (Phil. 2:5-8)

Once you fully let go of yourself, you take on the attitude of Christ Jesus. Jesus may have wanted the "cup" of suffering to be taken from Him (Matt. 26:39), but He went all the way to death to prove His trust in the Father's plans.

Many of us are familiar with Philippians 4:11, where Paul tells us he had "learned in whatever situation I am to be content." Notice the word *learned.* He did not just—poof!—understand contentment. He learned to be satisfied in God's private classroom of life. When Paul released what he wanted, he found gratification. Even when he was shipwrecked, beaten, and jailed for the sake of Christ, he found contentment. He learned to release his will, to die to his desires, and to live for Christ. "For to me to live is Christ, and to die is gain" (Phil. 1:21). Paul knew that death to self is truly living for Christ.

We cannot have godliness without contentment. "Now there is great gain in godliness *with* contentment" (1 Tim. 6:6, italics mine). The rich man in Luke 12:13-21 was not content with what he had. He planned to build more barns and have good years ahead of him. Yet that very night God required his soul. How much could he have done for the Lord had he found satisfaction with what he had? Unfortunately, we will never know. What a regretful statement. Often many of us are not content with our lot. When we are dissatisfied, we may be unable to see what God would want for us. This focus on ourselves keeps us from seeing God's blessings in our lives.

What We Deserve

Who are we to think we *deserve* marriage anyway? We don't deserve anything except judgment. God sent His Son to die on the cross so that we would have the hope of eternal life. We must find contentment in that hope. All we need or want should be wrapped up in the fact that the Heavenly Father provided a way for us to have eternal life with Him. We must repent of thinking that this season of our life is too hard or that anything in life is too difficult. God will not give us more than we can handle (1 Cor. 10:13; Phil. 4:13). God calls us to lay aside foolish and selfish thoughts, to press on, to push through, and to fight the good fight. God desires that we find contentment in Him alone. Once we come to a place where we lay aside our expectations of God, contentment will find us.

When you don't rid your heart of discontentment before marriage, it will creep up *within* your marriage. When you look to anything but God to bring you contentment and happiness, you will always be disappointed. One key piece of advice often given to people is to make sure they marry someone who is content with the Lord alone. Someone who enters into a marriage without being content with God alone may have a tendency to look to his or her mate as a "savior." That pressure can become overwhelming.

I knew a couple who found the idea of marriage so alluring that they rushed into it. The godly advice they received before marriage was to wait and slow down. Once married, they looked to each other for deep satisfaction and used each other as idols. A few years later they divorced. Sadly, this example is not unique.

Before marriage, both you and your future husband need to find contentment in Christ alone. Even then, don't work toward the goal of contentment so that God will then allow you to get married. God will not automatically say, "Okay, you're finally content. Now I will give you a mate." God's ways are not our ways, and He knows what is best for us. We just need to trust Him.

Being content with your singleness does not necessarily mean that God has blessed you with the gift of singleness either. Do not let contentment scare you. Making peace with singleness does not equal a life without the possibility of marriage. Being content means you are at peace—whether married or single. Once you achieve true contentment with our Lord and Savior, peace will follow.

Emotional Idols

Norm Wakefield states in his book *Equipped to Love*, "Whenever someone looks to anything or anyone rather than God as the source of all things, he commits the sin of idolatry. This may sound strange, but it's true. Here is a good definition of idolatry: looking to any person, object, or idea to supply what only God can supply." We must examine things in our lives that may be idols. Could it be the idea of marriage? Or could it be the close male friend you have?

Recently on Christian talk radio a counselor was helping people with their marital problems. A woman caller was desperate for answers and a quick fix for her persistent problem. She'd been married for ten years. She had befriended a Christian man on the Internet. Since she was not receiving emotional support from her husband, she turned to her computer friend. The emotions she needed from Mr. Internet prompted him to want a break in their relationship. This thought petrified the caller. She said, "I feel compelled to talk to him. I can't stop." She was looking for a "savior," someone to fill in the gaps that only God can fill. This Internet fling had become an idol in her life. Remember that an idol is anything you look to for something that only God can give you. The caller did not go into depth on the history of her marriage, but I can almost guarantee that during the start of her marriage she relied on her husband for the same things she now wanted from this Internet friend. She needed to go to her Heavenly Father for her emotional support and be content with Him.

Now, how does this relate to us? When discontentment is felt in life, when you don't find true contentment with God alone, problems can easily occur. Ask God to point out areas in your life where you are not content; then ask Him to help you be satisfied with His plan. He will begin to reveal areas where you are not fully in His will. Once this lesson is learned, you may need to lean on God the Educator to continue to keep you reminded of His instructions.

In an e-mail my newly-married friend Michelle explained this point quite well:

> I have learned that marriage does not quell my desires for stability or joy. But that is not a dig on marriage, or mine in particular, it is just to say that the Lord is supreme and His ways are to be desired above all. Because, let me tell you, with the Holy Spirit in you, you will *not* be satisfied even in a great marriage unless you are growing in your relationship with Jesus. He will not let you be happy with things of this earth. Now that I've led you to believe that my marriage is not satisfying all my desires . . . it is truly the most amazing blessing straight from heaven ('cause I could never do anything so perfect). He is so pure and unblemished and genuine and desiring to please me.

Michelle definitely understands that marriage is not the way to unending joy but is truly a blessing from God. She found contentment with Christ alone before marriage, and she sees her relationship with Him as crucial after marriage. She knows His plan is best.

chapter EIGHT

Trusting in God

DO YOU FEAR BEING SINGLE the rest of your life? Or do you fear being in a marriage not ordained by God? If the fear of being single is greater than the fear of being in the wrong marriage, problems will occur. I call these hysterical fears.

In 1 Peter 3:1-7 Peter addresses wives. He shares what women should strive for: "respectful and pure conduct" (v. 2), external beauty that reflects the internal beauty of "a gentle and quiet spirit" (vv. 3-4), and the adornment of submission (v. 5). Verse 6 states that we will become "children" of Sarah (Abraham's wife) if we "do good and do not *fear* anything that is frightening" (italics mine). We will achieve these godly qualities if we are not overcome by our hysterical fears.

Trusting God's Plan

Not trusting in God's plan can cause envy or discontent. However, let's look at some verses about God's ways compared to our ways:

> *The plans of the heart belong to man,*
> *but the answer of the tongue is from the LORD. (Prov. 16:1)*

As you do not know the way the spirit comes to the bones in the womb of a woman with child, so you do not know the work of God who makes everything. (Eccl. 11:5)

For my thoughts are not your thoughts,
neither are your ways my ways, declares the LORD.
For as the heavens are higher than the earth,
so are my ways higher than your ways
and my thoughts than your thoughts. (Isa. 55:8-9)

For I know the plans I have for you, declares the LORD. (Jer. 29:11a)

There are many more verses that speak about how God will direct us. At first we may not understand what God is doing, but we must trust Him. David said in Psalm 139:6, "Such knowledge is too wonderful for me; it is high; I cannot attain it." He was comfortable knowing that he did not know.

In time we may look back on our single years and see God's fingerprints everywhere. The pain, trials, and struggles become clear when we set envy aside. We will then see how the ups and downs of life are to be dealt with head on, free from envy.

We've all heard it said, "Hindsight is always 20/20." I think the children of Israel must have coined that phrase. Did they understand what God was going to do when they stood at the Red Sea with their enemies behind them (Exod. 14:10-29)? No. Did they understand or know where their food, water, and provision for their basic needs would come from (Exod. 15:22-27)? No. Did they understand what God would do when the spies reported that the land He gave to them was filled with giants (Num. 13:25-33)? No. They continued in their discontentment, and the cost became deadly.

The Israelites rebelled against God over and over in the wilderness, and often we do the same. The correlation between the children of Israel and us is clear: just as they were in bondage to the Egyptians, we are in bondage to believing that marriage is going to save us from this state of discontented singleness. God performed a grand exodus to save the Israelites from slavery; God sent His Son to save us from slavery. He led the Israelites through the wilderness of testing to worship and serve Him there, and He wants us to come through the wilderness of testing to see if we trust Him. Then He allowed the Israelites to enter the Promised Land. If you allow God to take you through the arid wilderness of trials, you will come through it trusting and obeying Him. The "Promised Land" is not marriage but rather a place of knowing that you are in the Father's hands and that you will not be single a day longer than He plans for you.

Recently I took inventory of how many single friends I have. There are not many left. Many have married and have begun to have children. Many of these girlfriends and I would sit around and talk about marriage and worry about when or if we were going to get married. We stirred the cauldron of hysterical fears all the way to the boiling point. Now many of them are married. What a waste of mental energy we spent on worry!

When a thought of discontentment, envy, or lack of trust comes into your head, pray. "Take every thought captive to obey Christ" (2 Cor. 10:5b). Let the Holy Spirit be your teacher (John 14:26). Let Him provide the learning environment. The pain from this hot desert of the Lord's testing is His hand conforming you to His likeness.

Also, read verses about God's goodness and His promises for your life. Let these awesome promises from the Father comfort you:

May the LORD give strength to his people!
May the LORD bless his people with peace! (Ps. 29:11)

They who wait for the LORD shall renew their strength;
they shall mount up with wings like eagles;
they shall run and not be weary;
they shall walk and not faint. (Isa. 40:31)

The LORD will guide you continually
and satisfy your desire in scorched places
and make your bones strong;
and you shall be like a watered garden,
like a spring of water,
whose waters do not fail. (Isa. 58:11)

Bring the full tithes into the storehouse, that there may be food in my house.
And thereby put me to the test, says the LORD of hosts, if I will not open the
windows of heaven for you and pour down for you a blessing until there is no
more need. (Mal. 3:10)

Do not be anxious about anything, but in everything by prayer and supplication with thanksgiving let your requests be made known to God. And the peace of God, which surpasses all understanding, will guard your hearts and your minds in Christ Jesus. (Phil. 4:6-7)

My God will supply every need of yours according to his riches in glory in Christ Jesus. (Phil. 4:19)

Can you understand that being envious and not trusting God can create a wall between you and the Father? Does it excite you to be at a place of peace about your singleness? Our God is very giving, and we have no business seeking to please our wills (our flesh). Only He can satisfy the deepest longings of our souls. Throw off your envy and discontentment, fall on your knees, and trust in an all-loving, all-powerful, completely organized, and totally faithful God.

chapter NINE

Creating Safe Ideals

DO YOU KNOW ANYONE WHO thinks marriage is the best prize in life? Maybe you feel marriage would elevate you to a newer, higher level. Has this thought ever crept into your mind: *If I was married, I would be happy. If I had a husband and children—my own family to nurture—I would be happy.*

An underlying, unspoken feeling in Christian circles seems to be that marriage brings you to a deeper level of spirituality. It is almost as though marriage is the pinnacle of the Christian life.

In *Common Mistakes Singles Make*, Mary Whelchel backs up this train of thought:

> There is a very common tendency to think that life hasn't really begun for us yet. We're just marking time, flying around in a holding pattern, waiting for this prerequisite—marriage—before life can truly start. Even though many singles protest that they aren't doing this, they are.

Christian Ideal

As Christians, we have this ideal of a Christian marriage: husbands loving their wives as Christ loves the church and wives being submissive to their husbands. We see marriage as a means to unending companionship and deep intimacy. Marriage *is* a place for companionship and intimacy, but when we experiment with satisfying those desires on our own, we will be let down. Tracy found in Mike a deep friendship, and he made her feel a certain way. However, when Tracy finally says, "I do," will her husband satisfy her emotional needs the same as Mike did? What if he cannot satisfy them as well as Mike? What if she never feels as connected emotionally with her husband as she did with Mike? She will continually compare the two, and this comparison can lead to discontentment in her marriage.

If I were to compare all my married friends, I would have to say that overall my non-Christian friends are more content in their marriages than my Christian friends. As I mentioned earlier, a person who enters into marriage not fully content in the Lord may look to his or her spouse to provide contentment. But remember, God does not allow anything except Himself to make us fully content. So my non-Christian friends marry with much lower expectations as to how their mate will satisfy their needs. In a recent conversation with a married, Christian girlfriend about this issue, she said her expectations were high going into her marriage. When her mate did not prove to be the exact copy of what the Bible says about a husband, she had to look to God to find peace. It proved to be a struggle between her heart and head.

Among my happily married Christian friends, I see a common thread. First, they each went into marriage with an attitude of giving 110 percent, not with a "what can I gain from this?" attitude. Second, their hearts were thankful to have someone with whom to worship and serve God. Third, they had realistic expectations. They did not depend on their mates to be a vending machine of emotions and actions they could throw their change into and have personal desires met. Commitment, communication, and Christ made up their formula to make their marriage God-honoring.

A Safe Haven

What makes the prize-of-life-attitude worse is that older Christians feed this lie. They seem to pity the single and revere the married. My sister went through a Bible study workbook with our aunt, who is not much older than her. The study was titled *Homemaking*. Since our aunt is married, she asked if they could study some issues that might be helpful for her. When they opened the book, they read this sentence from the chapter called "Your Divine Task": "Marriage ushers in a safe haven after the loneliness and problems of single life." What kind of statement is that!

A safe haven with no more loneliness? I have married friends who would say this statement does not describe their marriages. Yes, marriage should provide a safe haven, and your mate does provide companionship, but there are times in a marriage when couples may experience both insecurity and loneliness. Marriage in and of itself will not bring about satisfaction or solutions to your problems. God is the only One who can do that.

Physical Intimacy

Another factor that contributes to this attitude of elevating marriage to an idolatrous status is physical intimacy. Most Christians desire to be virgins on their wedding day. (It breaks my heart that I have not known many who before marriage fulfilled this part of God's plan in this aspect of becoming man and wife. May God's Word pierce our hearts and drive us to remain pure.) When a couple becomes involved physically but want to wait until their wedding night to complete the sex act, they place a great deal of emphasis on the act itself. Each time they have to restrain themselves and not complete the act that God created, they continue to build the idea that marriage will allow the freedom to go "all the way."

Most married couples say that physical intimacy is a small part of marriage. Yet for some reason the permission to have sex after wedding vows have been spoken is conveyed in our Christian culture to be one of the most important aspects of marriage. I have heard a few engaged Christian men say, "Only x amount of days until it is legal!" or "After we are married I can have it as much as I want."

There *is* physical freedom in marriage. Yet too often that is the only special territory left to await marriage. When we are already emotionally and spiritually intimate, the only act to complete the marriage union is sexual intercourse. This is not how God wants it to be. If we vow to remain pure physically, emotionally, and spiritually before marriage, this will leave much uncharted territory to discover after marriage. Physical intimacy will not be the only undiscovered area. Wouldn't it be exciting to know that you and your spouse will have many new discoveries to make together? And that your spouse hasn't had the same discoveries with an ex-girlfriend or even a "good friend"? That is exciting to me! That is true romance.

This may scare the living daylights out of some of you because it raises many questions: *What if we never connect on that deep level after marriage? What if our feelings never measure up to what I think they should? What if I never have those feelings of love that you suggest I save? What if we are not physically compatible? What if . . . ?* Ask yourself this question: Is God cruel? If you are asking God for a kind, gentle, considerate mate, do you think He will give you a mean, insensitive, rude mate? God is not out there planning how to make you miserable. When you obey Him, He blesses you. We do not serve a malicious God who will pull a fast one on us.

> *Ask, and it will be given to you; seek, and you will find; knock, and it will be opened to you. For everyone who asks receives, and the one who seeks finds, and to the one who knocks it will be opened. Or which one of you, if his son asks him for bread, will give him a stone? . . . If you then, who are evil, know how to give good gifts to your children, how much more will your Father who is in heaven give good things to those who ask him!* (Matt. 7:7-11)

Let that encourage you.

Never Left Alone

Next to salvation, your choice of a mate is the biggest decision of your life. God is not going to leave you hanging. Marriage is created to paint a picture of our relationship with Him. He desires your marriage to bring Him glory. Satan, on the other hand, loves to rob you of your faith and trust. Satan plays mind games and wants you to think you need to do things the way the world does things in order to find happiness. But we find our joy in Christ and not in the things of this world.

How much did you know about the Christian walk and faith when you began your lifelong commitment to God? You didn't know much; you relied on your faith. No matter how much you tried to know about Christ before you committed to Him, it boiled down to pure faith. Why do you feel you need to know it *all* before you make a commitment in a relationship? Where is your faith on this issue? It may take gut-wrenching faith to save your emotions for your mate; it also takes gut-wrenching faith to commit yourself to God.

Is your testimony like the woman's next to you? No. Coming into a relationship with God is different for each of us, but the conclusion is the same. Likewise with marriage. All of our paths to meeting our spouses may look different, but in the end we are married.

The prize of life is a relationship with our Creator. To look to anything else to fill that gap will not bring about satisfaction. God designed marriage, but He also designed us to be complete when we are with Him. Marriage is not the answer to eternal bliss. To give it that much credit is taking away credit from the Creator. Marriage is *a* blessing, not *the* blessing! A deeper walk with the Lord is not to be brought about by marriage alone but by reading His Word, talking to Him, obeying Him, and giving Him praise, glory, and honor.

chapter TEN

Watching Your Feelings

WE HAVE BECOME A CULTURE absorbed with feelings. It's what we do with our feelings and whom we turn to for relief that makes the difference. God has feelings such as jealousy, grief, joy, sorrow, friendliness, etc. God, the Creator of all, created emotions.

Feelings have become great foundations for stories and characters. In *Sense and Sensibility* by Jane Austen, two sisters express their feelings in opposite manners. The older sister Emma keeps a tight rein on her feelings, until the end when she breaks down and releases every pent-up emotion. The other sister, on the other hand, is fancy-free with her emotions, expressing them even at the pain of others. Throughout the novel and movie we see the positive and negative effects of each sister's method of controlling or not controlling her emotions.

The subplot of my story of Tracy and Mike is what she felt about Mike. Feelings are a large part of our lives, but as some say, can you trust them?

Types of Feelings

As singles we seem to have feelings running wild through our veins. We pulse with loneliness, frustration, envy, confusion, and a host of other uncomfortable feelings. Being single can bring on a set of emotions that dash ahead of our rational thoughts. God gave us the ability to feel and love, but when we focus on how we feel, we may lose sight of why God gave us this human capacity.

Let's look at two of the many types of feelings we have the ability to experience.

We have *foundational feelings*. These feelings are answers to our deep questions such as: What is the meaning of life? What is my purpose? A believer should have a fundamental sense of who he or she is according to God. The goal of a believer is to "love the Lord your God with all your heart and with all your soul and with all your mind" (Matt. 22:37). A person who does not know God, or is not known by God, holds no answers to these questions. God put eternity into people's hearts (Eccl. 3:11), and once we know we have eternal life, this void is satisfied in our hearts. Many have heard that we have a God-shaped vacuum in our hearts; when we come to know Him, this empty vacuum is filled. Our identity in Christ provides us peaceful feelings deep in our hearts. These resulting deep foundational feelings of hope for eternal life (Titus 1:2; 3:7) should not waver according to our situation, thoughts, attitudes, or moods.

God's written will for our life can be compared to these foundational feelings. We read His will for us in His Word in statements such as "Do not lay up for yourselves treasures on earth" (Matt. 6:19a) or "do not be anxious about your life" (Matt. 6:25a). God's will for our lives is unchanging and will not waver based on situations, thoughts, attitudes, or moods. So these foundational feelings of who we are—"a chosen race, a royal priesthood, a holy nation, a people for his own possession" (1 Pet. 2:9)—should not waver. God's Word provides a constant, stable base of peace at the core of our souls.

Another type of feeling we experience is *surface feelings*. These change daily and are reactions to what may be going on in our hearts. For example, we find out a friend is having a baby, and we feel joy and excitement. We step onto a roller coaster, and we feel scared and anxious. We start a new job, and we feel awkward and clumsy. We see a wedding on TV, and we feel envious and frustrated. In life things come our way, and our surface feelings change depending on the situations. Have you ever seen a movie that takes you from crying to laughing, from frustration to peace? To run the gamut of all emotions is not uncommon in a movie, and it can leave us drained of any feelings.

Just as our foundational feelings reflect God's written will, our surface feelings may be compared to God's plan for our lives. God's plan for individual lives is not written in black and white. Each day we seek to find what He would want us to do and to obey step by step. For example, you may be considering a job transfer. God's written Word says to work hard (Col. 3:23) and not to be in debt to anyone (Rom. 13:8), among other things. If the job transfer lines up with God's written Word, you should seek Him through prayer, asking Him for wisdom and listening to the prompting of the Holy Spirit. God's plan for our lives may shift, but it will never contradict His written will. In the same way, our surface feelings will change, but they should not disagree with our foundational sense of who we are in the Lord.

Jealousy

Christian singles, both men and women, have a look of, "Hey, I'm single. I don't like it, and I won't be happy until I'm married!" Rarely will they verbalize this to anyone, but their actions speak volumes. These feelings manifest themselves in different ways. It could be a roll of the eyes at a loving couple or it may be restrained, such as a root of bitterness lurking in the heart.

Once while I searched for a job, a close friend of mine was hired as a flight attendant. I was jealous, mainly because she knew where God wanted her to work. My heart said, *You are employed, and I don't like it. Why is God keeping me in the dark right now regarding the direction of my life?* Of course, when she would talk excitedly about her future I would fake my happiness for her. Then the Holy Spirit convicted me with Romans 12:15a: "Rejoice with those who rejoice." I wasn't really rejoicing with her—I was only pretending. I immediately went to my friend and asked her to forgive me. The mask I wore was a massive façade, hiding a covetous heart full of envy.

This wasn't about being jealous of someone's marital status but of something someone had that I wanted. Our own hearts can deceive us. Our hearts can lie, which may cause us to ignore what we are really feeling. Then in order to cover up pain, frustration, or sadness we put on a show. If we put on a show of happiness, excitement, or joy when our feelings are the opposite, we are lying, and that is not a good thing. Being honest with my friend led to a life lesson that helped me to understand that I must be content where God has me at the moment. I have no right to think He loves my brothers and sisters in Christ more than me just because they have a job, a mate, or anything else I think I deserve.

Pretending

Another way feelings cause difficulty is when a person makes it clear that he or she is available. That person may even come across to others as different than who he or she really is in order to appear as marriage material. How might you do this? Perhaps by laughing loudly at a prospect's joke, agreeing with ideas or actions you're not totally comfortable with, or sharing how God is teaching and growing you with the hope of attracting a mate who is impressed by your godly character and qualities. This is acting and manipulating, putting on a show—and it's wrong. I have seen it. I have done it. We can all be good actors when there is someone to impress.

I'll make a confession here to help you fully understand what I am saying. One night I attended a picnic that a male single prospect also attended. I wanted him to see that I have a heart for serving. So I jumped up as soon as I finished eating and picked up plates, did dishes, stacked chairs, and emptied trash. Why did I do this? I hoped that this man would see me as a good servant of the Lord. Again Heather learned a life lesson. Not only did he not notice me—*no one* noticed I was such a good helper! This was what I call a "Hello, Heather!" moment. The Holy Spirit said, "Hello, Heather. When you are serving to please man, how can you please God?" (see Gal. 1:10).

This is the category Tracy found herself in. Tracy did not tell anyone she thought she would be married by now. She opened up to Mike beyond her comfort level in hopes of being more attractive to him, thereby putting her timing above God's timing.

When there is the possibility of a relationship turning into marriage, all our unpleasant feelings about relationships or values can get lost in the back of the closet, only to resurface when the "friendship" turns out like Tracy and Mike's. Tracy may have found contentment with where God had her at the moment because she tasted what she wanted, but those ugly feelings would only return when their friendship ended.

Sad Singles

We all know single people who present their sad case of singleness to all their friends. They make sure everyone knows they are on the hunt for that special someone. They scan the "Personals" section in the newspaper hoping to find "the one." Or they register with Christian online dating services that encourage participants to post their picture and a short bio to attract Mr. Right. (I do not think all online dating services are bad. However, when someone uses one out of pure desperation, she may lower her normal standard just to catch a date.) These unmarried people seem to flaunt their empty ring finger and mention to everyone their intense desire to be married. The desire to be married is not wrong, but how you react to the desire can overshadow your service to the Lord.

In the situations mentioned above, your feelings about not being married can change based on how others respond to your complaints about "single life insecurities." Well-meaning friends will say things to heal a lonely heart, such as "You will make a great wife" or "Keep looking—he has to be out there somewhere." People will feed into this idea that marriage will quench emptiness, when in reality only looking to the Source will satisfy.

Many people involved in a singles group will feed into each other. They can become so wrapped up in their singleness, that is all they study or talk about. Yes, talking about and understanding the journey through the single years should help us focus more on serving the Lord, but obsessing about it will only lead to further discontentment.

I have seen friends who keep themselves busy to avoid feelings of loneliness and dissatisfaction. Hurrying to work, to Bible study, to the gym, to lunch, to a weekend here, to a weekend there, to the movies, to the bowling alley, to church, to choir, to a coffee shop, to praise band practice, to the Post Office, to the laundromat, to the grocery store, to the bank, to the car wash . . . the list goes on. Do you feel as though you are in a whirlwind?

Most of these activities are important but should be kept in their proper place. The things we do should not be used as a method to avoid obeying what God wants for us. Nor should we bury unwanted feelings in schedules full of hectic activity.

I'll add to the list of deterrents. Sleeping too much, overeating, under-eating, excessive spending, smoking, overexercise, gossiping, disproportionate working, gambling, drunkenness, pornography, romance novels, unhealthy relationships, obsessive self-focus, and a host of other things can keep us from facing what we feel. Some people turn to alcohol to drift off to dreamland and forget reality, but we could use any of the above-mentioned activities to do the same thing. We are flesh, and in our flesh we have a tendency to look for worldly things and activities to keep us happy.

Let God Be God

> *Search me, O God, and know my heart!*
> *Try me and know my thoughts!*
> *And see if there be any grievous way in me,*
> *and lead me in the way everlasting! (Ps. 139:23-24)*

When you keep busy to avoid something, you may not have time to be quiet before God. He asks us to "Be still, and know that I am God" (Ps. 46:10a). One reason for this is to quiet our hearts and let Him examine our deepest layers. God wants to be the God of our feelings. Our only task is to let Him be God. When we step ahead, we get in His way. God gives deliverance from ungodly emptiness or lonely feelings.

Let's take the example of my friend with the job as a flight attendant and my waiting on God's direction. The Holy Spirit sometimes speaks in a whisper; so when our lives and minds are busy, it can be hard to hear His voice. Let's say I faked being happy for her and kept myself busy with activities to squelch my feelings of envy. I may have searched harder for a job and resented her without being able to fully understand why. This resentment could have grown until I truly disliked her. I could have become bitter toward God and then one day wondered why I felt that way. Thankfully, my heart found peace, I heard the Holy Spirit, and He taught me the lesson He meant for me to learn.

Finding satisfaction is a beautiful thing. The root reasons for feeling incomplete or unsatisfied are that we are not relying on the foundational feelings of who we are in Christ and are being discontent with where God has us.

What God Thinks

Why do we allow our surface feelings to dictate happiness or sadness, satisfaction or disappointment? This may be caused by our tendency to forget our true identity. Take a few moments and read out loud the list below with descriptions from the Word of what God thinks of you.

- I am a person for God's own possession (1 Pet. 2:9).
- I am God's child, and I call Him Abba (Father) (Rom. 8:15).
- I am redeemed through Christ and have forgiveness (Eph. 1:7).
- God loves me, and I am precious in His sight (Isa. 43:4).
- I am lifted and carried by God through all trials (Isa. 63:9).

Surface feelings can be changed, heightened, or numbed by our surroundings and by the things we watch, read, or talk about. When we rely on our feelings of dissatisfaction to determine how we will act or think, we toss God's Word and His power aside.

The list above is in no way a complete catalog of all of the references of God's feelings toward you. As you continue to study the Word, ask God to reveal all that's mentioned there about His loving, tender feelings toward you, and then rely on *those* feelings. Know that God is the One who satisfies and makes you complete.

Spend time before Him, and quiet your heart. Allow God to show you how He feels about you. Seek Him first, not a mate. Give Him your heart, and His blessings will follow your obedience.

Learning to manage your unruly feelings may be difficult at first, but as you realize that God is the God of all feelings, it will become easier. He wants you to place all your hopes and feelings in the palm of His hand and leave them there for His use. As you strive toward a deeper level of trust with your emotions, waiting for His timing will be a beautiful season in your spiritual life.

chapter ELEVEN

Understanding Your Expectations

HAVE YOU EVER MADE PLANS for a day of shopping? You want to go here and there, enjoy lunch at a special restaurant, and end the day at the local theater. But when you meet up with your shopping partner, she has a different set of plans. She wants to eat at a fast-food joint, shop at only one mall, and definitely does not want to see a movie. What does this do to your expectations? It shoots them down. At that point you have two ways to react: selfishly or unselfishly. You can go off into the world of annoyance and disappointment, or you can accept what is before you and go on with life.

We expect all kinds of things from all kinds of people in all kinds of ways. We expect people waiting on us at the store to be kind and attentive. We expect our food to be served quickly at a restaurant. We expect our boss to give us a big raise. We expect our mom to always be there for us. We expect our friends to know better. Life is full of expectations. What we need to know is how we react when our expectations are not met. What makes or breaks us in the situation? And even more, how does our behavior affect another person's expectations?

Pride

When we cling to our expectations, we are saying we know what should happen or what would be best in a given situation. This is pride. Any time we believe we hold the keys to what would be best in any circumstance, we act like some kind of god. Eve thought she knew what would be best, and look what happened!

When I find myself frustrated, angry, annoyed, or having a stinky attitude, it's because of an unfulfilled expectation. This nips at me all the time. Learning to set aside unmet expectations unselfishly can be difficult.

You may have had the thought, *I should be married by now.* Or, *How can so-and-so be married and not me?* When you place an expectation on a situation and it is not met, the flesh has a tendency to take over. This expectation attitude allows Satan to get a foothold in our minds and causes us to not trust God.

> For the weapons of our warfare are not of the flesh but have divine power to destroy strongholds. We destroy arguments and every lofty opinion raised against the knowledge of God, and we take every thought captive to obey Christ. (2 Cor. 10:4-5)

This is a powerful verse when it comes to allowing our expectations to not rule over reality or rational thought. If you look up *stronghold* in some dictionaries, you will find definitions such as "vise-like grip," "monopoly," "stranglehold," and "iron grip." Wow! How wonderful to know that when we put on our divine armor we can literally throw down Satan. His schemes cannot keep us locked up!

Strongholds

Our Lord and Savior has broken the chains of the destructive strongholds. Strongholds, such as looking to marriage to "save us," are broken only through the power of Jesus. We have to believe and pray that God will allow us to "lay aside every weight, and sin which clings so closely, and let us run with endurance the race that is set before us, looking to Jesus, the founder and perfecter of our faith" (Heb. 12:1b-2a).

Have you felt at times that things in your life keep you mentally weighed down? Have you felt that spiritual pull on your mind? At those times you are not tapped into the Source, who can with a simple blow destroy those chains that bind.

We must renew our minds daily if we are going to have a renewing of our reactions to unmet expectations. "If then you have been raised with Christ, seek the things that are above, where Christ is, seated at the right hand of God. Set your minds on things that are above, not on things that are on earth" (Col. 3:1-2).

When you commit your life to Christ, you should strive to set your mind on Him and on heavenly realities. Paul tells us here to keep seeking the things that are above, to keep moving forward. Ephesians 4:15 states, "We are to grow up in every way into him who is the head, into Christ." This process of renewing is ongoing, and with God's help you will grow closer to Him.

You might protest, "Hey, I have tried to take captive every thought and set my mind on things above, and it just doesn't work. I still feel cheated by God in the marriage department—He never allows me to have what I want." When you have a thought not focused on God or not honoring God or when you expect something that does not come, what do you do? Do you allow it to grow and fester in your mind? Do you dwell on the unattainable? This is where the battle begins.

Inner Thoughts and Emotions

Okay, my friend, this may be hard to explain because it deals with the inner thoughts and motives of people. Each one of us has to ask God what honors Him.

> *Finally, brothers, whatever is true, whatever is honorable, whatever is just, whatever is pure, whatever is lovely, whatever is commendable, if there is any excellence, if there is anything worthy of praise, think about these things. (Phil. 4:8)*

These are the things God desires us to think upon. Keeping our thoughts pure will help us keep our emotions pure.

When I desired a relationship with a male friend, I would go over imaginary conversations in my head. My expectation elevated with each fantasized *téte-à-téte*. Was this honoring God? I would say no. Reread Philippians 4:8—"Whatever is true . . ." Were these chats true? No; it was Heather wasting mental energy on relational fantasies.

Tracy's heart could have been spared pain if she had avoided thinking Mike was going to return her feelings. She allowed herself to read into too many of Mike's actions. She also had Emma feeding into the Mike saga. Had she taken captive each thought about Mike and their potential future, her heart would have been more protected. Our minds have become battlefields. We need to recognize the battle and declare war.

Once war is declared, we need to come up with battle plans. My plan was this: When I found myself drifting to the world of make-believe, I told myself, *Take captive every thought to the obedience of Christ.* This helped a great deal, and before I knew it I was no longer wasting mental energy on bogus conversations. My friend told me she would say to herself, *Take captive every thought to the obedience of Christ, and soon you'll be thinking of something nice.* This rhyme helped her stay focused.

Women, you know what I mean when it comes to controlling our emotional thoughts. A well-meaning Christian male befriends you, and before you know it, out of the blue, wedding plans burst into your thoughts, and your name, transformed to Mrs. His-Last-Name, repeats itself in your wandering mind. Can't you just hear Tracy thinking, *Mrs. Michael Hartman*? Raise your hand if you have ever been guilty of this mindless exercise. I have no doubt that all hands are raised.

I want to share a story about a friend who struggled with such thoughts. She had recently joined a singles group and befriended a young man who went on an extended mission trip not long after they met. During the trip he wrote her letters to share with the whole group. One week she received a letter that included one for the group and one for her. On the top of the page he had written "For you only" in large print.

The letter opened with the common basic pleasantries of asking how she was and typical small talk. Then came, "Hey . . . I just wanted you to know I think that it is neat you are taking such a major step in ministry. I just want you to be encouraged that I am behind you 100 percent. I'll continue to pray for you and look forward to seeing how God uses you. If you ever need anything, know that I am there for you. Maybe we can run a couple of [camping] trips this fall. Love in Christ."

You might think this letter was an innocent letter of encouragement, but my friend struggled with not thinking more of this young man than just a brother in Christ. She expected there to be more of a relationship between them. However, when he came home, God showed her that this man was not to be her husband. She had wasted a lot of her emotions and mental energy.

Meaningful Friends

How can we as sisters in Christ help each other with our own personal battlefields? We must be aware of how we feed into the unknown with each other. Remember Emma? She added plenty of fuel to the fire that was growing inside Tracy's heart. Emma tried to keep a positive spin on the relationship. She meant well, but she was naive.

When a girlfriend starts to talk "hypothetically" about a possible relationship with a guy, what is your reaction? Do you keep it real? Or do you build up the notion that this relationship will happen?

I'll admit I have participated in more than one of these conversations. I have been "Emma" to several of my girlfriends. It is easy to become wrapped up with relationship, marriage, and guy talk. However, when the Lord started to reveal to me the importance of emotional purity, these conversations ended as quickly as they started.

Let's help each other maintain an accurate perspective. We can be each other's greatest weapons for fighting this battle in our minds.

Dangerous Passages

Thinking unrealistic and make-believe thoughts can become a vicious cycle. Mental strife can lead to "striving after wind" (Eccl. 1:14b), which is futile. When a fantasy starts, you need to combat it with the Word and take captive every thought to the obedience of Jesus Christ. I do not mean ungodly fantasies (though we need to combat those also), but the ones about a conversation you would love to have with a special person, the things you could do together, the jokes you could tell, the sunsets you could enjoy, how great marriage would be, how you would feel in a wedding dress . . . the list goes on. Of course, having a hope of all these things is not the problem. The problem is when this hope turns into a mental stronghold or when focus on these hopes outweighs your focus on God. Each of these fantasies or expectations can lead to self-focus and self-pity.

Thought Control

In a nutshell this requires self-control of the mind. When you "walk by the Spirit . . . you will not gratify the desires of the flesh. For the desires of the flesh are against the Spirit, and the desires of the Spirit are against the flesh, for these are opposed to each other . . . the fruit of the Spirit is . . . self-control" (Gal. 5:16-17, 22-23).

God knew people would indulge their minds. "Among whom we all *once lived* in the passions of our flesh, *carrying out* the desires of the body and the *mind*" (Eph. 2:3, italics mine).

This indulgence needs to be done away with when we become new in Him. Again remember that Paul told the Philippians to think on "whatever is true . . . honorable . . . just . . . pure . . . lovely . . . commendable . . . any excellence . . . anything worthy of praise" (Phil. 4:8). Thinking on these things will keep our expectations in line with the Word.

If you do not learn to control your thoughts as a single person, they will be even more difficult to control once you're married. Whether you are a man or a woman, your thought life must be under control before marriage or it will haunt you afterward.

Women, if you let yourself become wrapped up in your expectations, and then your husband does not live up to your expectations when you are married, these ungodly fantasies may reappear. Maybe this scenario could help.

A married woman feels emotionally distant from her husband. She'd thought that once she was married she'd never be lonely again. She does not know where that closeness went, but she longs to feel emotionally connected to someone. The new pastor starts counseling her to help unravel these feelings. The pastor maintains healthy boundaries, never becoming personal with her. He helps her uncover problems in her marriage. During their sessions the woman starts to notice the small details the pastor remembers and the way he is sensitive to her needs. Before she knows what is happening, her mind cannot stop thinking about the pastor. When he preaches, she thinks of the positive qualities he possesses that her husband lacks. Now her expectations for her husband have become an emotional mountain he will never be able to scale. Discontentment wreaks havoc though every fiber of her being—all because she was unable to keep her thoughts in check.

I have met or received e-mails from married women across the country who have struggled with this very issue. A homeschooling mom with eight kids confessed her growing obsession with a man she'd met in a chat room on the Internet. Her husband had grown "emotionally distant," and her friend on the Internet filled the void. After hearing about emotional purity, she realized how this relationship went against what the Lord had for her and her marriage. She wrote me to not only share her story but to agree with the concept of finding and maintaining emotional purity before and *after* marriage.

We must strive toward complete contentment with the life God has given us. Each season of life will present opportunities for growth, and we should long for God to enroll us in His private school. Unmet expectations are a part of life, and knowing how to deal with them in a godly fashion is an excellent skill to learn.

Reaction

We need to keep our own feelings and expectations in line with what God says. Also, we must not invoke feelings or raise expectations in another person when there is no commitment to take the relationship to another level. We need to be careful how others could perceive our actions.

When a guy friend pays special attention to us, such as inviting us to his folks' home for Sunday dinner, calling just to chat, sharing dreams, sharing struggles, or simply setting us apart from others, what does that do to our hearts? It usually gets us dreaming of the land of marriage and temporarily fills our emotional needs. Men need to realize how emotionally charged women are and should avoid causing them to imagine more than what is really there. Men can also be emotionally charged by the actions of a well-meaning friend. We all have to be pure in our actions toward our brothers and sisters in the Lord.

Recently I explained this concept to a Christian brother. He understood when I said women are as emotionally charged as men are visually charged. He said, "Oh, so a woman can be emotionally married like a man can be visually married in his mind." A beautiful light-bulb moment!

We have to be aware of how others react to our actions. "Therefore let us . . . decide never to put a stumbling block or hindrance in the way of a brother" (Rom. 14:13). It is acceptable in this society to have a "that's their problem" mind-set, but the Word teaches us the complete opposite.

We each have an important role when it comes to how we present ourselves to others. Mike should have been aware that his playful nudges, tight hugs, and soft pecks were causing Tracy to feel as though she were someone special to him. His actions suggested there was more to the friendship, but his words "We're just great friends" showed his true feelings.

I have heard that a man can undress a woman in his mind in less than ten seconds. Well, a woman can be emotionally married in her mind in less than ten seconds. Both men and women need to strive toward purity in all that they do and say to each other.

How to

So let's get practical—how can we do this? It's pretty simple. Avoid treating friends of the opposite sex as special. Treat them as you would anyone else. How did Mike treat Emma differently than Tracy? He treated her in no unusual manner. He never sought her out in a crowd. He didn't call her to just chat. Playful nudges were not part of their friendship, and neither were soft pecks good-bye after a holiday weekend with the folks.

Why was it wrong for Tracy and Mike to raise each other's expectations? They used each other to gain something they needed—friendship, companionship, a workout buddy, emotional connection, or even worse, a feeling of satisfaction. They defrauded, or took advantage of, each other. We should examine how we act toward those around us and should treat them with honesty in ways that will not summon any feelings or expectations that we cannot righteously satisfy.

Also, being able react to your brothers in Christ (and their unmet expectations and ungodly thoughts) with self-control of the mind and actions will be a testimony that God is at work in your life. He longs for us to give our minds to Him. He is the only source of fulfillment. Until we truly understand this, we will look for other things to satisfy us. When our mind finds freedom from wasted mental energy, we can abide in the peace and joy of God.

Stop Satan dead in his tracks, and fix your mind on Jesus. Have an intense gaze upon Him (Heb. 12:1-2), and all your ways will be established. Lay your feelings and expectations on His altar, and allow Him to be your sole Provider, Comforter, and Companion.

This poem, apparently written by Russell Kelfer and included in his book *Wait: A Journey to Discovering the Heart of God*, is a beautiful work that reflects the dialogue that many of us have with our Maker when we are feeling frustrated with the quietness of His voice.

Wait

Desperately, helplessly, longingly, I cried:
Quietly, patiently, lovingly God replied.
I pled and I wept for a clue to my fate,
And the Master so gently said,
"Child, you must wait."
"Wait? You say, wait!" my indignant reply.
"Lord, I need answers, I need to know why!
Is Your hand shortened? Or have You not heard?
By faith, I have asked, and am claiming Your Word.

"My future and all to which I can relate
Hangs in the balance, and You tell me to WAIT?
I'm needing a 'Yes,' a go-ahead sign,
Or even a 'No' to which I can resign.

"And Lord, You promised that if we believe
We need but to ask, and we shall receive.
And, Lord, I've been asking, and this is my cry:
'I'm weary of asking! I need a reply!'"

Then quietly, softly, I learned of my fate
As my Master replied once again, "You must wait."
So, I slumped in my chair, defeated and taut
And grumbled to God, "So, I'm waiting . . . for what?"

He seemed, then, to kneel
And His eyes wept with mine,
And He tenderly said, "I could give you a sign.

emotional PURITY

I could shake the heavens, and darken the sun.
I could raise the dead, and cause mountains to run.

"All you seek, I could give, and pleased you would be.
You would have what you want—
But, you wouldn't know Me.
You'd not know the depth of My love for each saint;
You'd not know the power I give to the faint;

"You'd not learn to see through the clouds of despair;
You'd not learn to trust just by knowing I'm there;
You'd not know the joy of resting in Me;
When darkness and silence were all you could see.

"You'd never experience that fullness of love
As the peace of My Spirit descends like a dove;
You'd know that I give and I save, for a start,
But you'd not know the depth of the beat of My heart.

"The glow of My comfort late into the night,
The faith that I give when you walk without sight,
The depth that's beyond getting just what you asked
Of an infinite God, who makes what you have last.

"You'd never know, should your pain quickly flee,
What it means that, 'My grace is sufficient for thee.'
Yes, your dreams for your loved one overnight would come true,
But, oh, the loss if I lost what I'm doing in you!

"So, be silent, My child, and in time you will see
That the greatest of gifts is to get to know Me.
And though oft' may My answers seem terribly late,
My most precious answer of all is still, 'Wait.'"

chapter TWELVE

Following God's Plan

I want you to be free from anxieties. The unmarried man is anxious about the things of the Lord, how to please the Lord. . . . And the unmarried or betrothed woman is anxious about the things of the Lord, how to be holy in body and spirit. . . . I say this for your own benefit, not to lay any restraint upon you, but to promote good order and to secure your undivided devotion to the Lord.
(1 Cor. 7:32, 34–35)

SECURE YOUR UNDIVIDED DEVOTION to the Lord." Briefly consider these few meaty words. It sounds simple; yet living it out in our daily lives may prove to be a stiff assignment. In our society, keeping ourselves "anxious about the things of the Lord" has taken on many definitions, especially when applied to singles.

Me, Myself, and I

Why do so many unmarried people have a hard time facing their singleness head-on? Mainly it's because many singles keep themselves wrapped up in activities that do not foster a love relationship with Christ. They do things they want to do (selfishness) without counting the cost that will be paid. They live in the here and now. This focus on self permeates this life stage, and for many the years of being single become a wasteland of me, myself, and I, with little concern about serving and enjoying God.

Mary Whelchel puts it plainly in her book *Common Mistakes Singles Make:*

> Let's face it, when you are single . . . it's not difficult to become self-focused. Who else do you really have to consider but yourself? If a

single person is not involved in reaching out to other people, that lack of accountability or responsibility to others can produce a selfish lifestyle.

When singles keep their attention or energy focused on themselves and not on a love relationship with God, they miss out on many activities that would bring about deep satisfaction. Enjoying and serving the Creator should be our number one goal, and this period in our life allows for 100 percent attention on God. Remember Paul's statement of fact: "But the married man is anxious about worldly things, how to please his wife . . . the married woman is anxious about . . . how to please her husband" (1 Cor. 7:33-34).

We ought to rejoice for this time of undistracted fellowship. This undivided attention to the Lord is the *point* of single life. To use this season in our lives to focus on self does not prepare us for the daily putting aside of self that takes place in marriage. Maybe this is why 50 percent of marriages fail. When someone promotes self before marriage, that person will still promote self after the wedding. When do you think you are going to learn to be unselfish?

In an e-mail a newly-married girlfriend, Michelle, shared a bit of insight with me. "I will never forget when April [her sister] told me three years ago that if I was preparing myself for marriage, I should practice being selfless. Very true—there is simply no room for selfishness in a marriage that is to endure years and changes."

Since marriage requires laying aside our will and serving another, why not learn this in our single years? If we compare people who spend their single years focusing on themselves to people who are focusing on God, do you think they would look different? You better believe it! Understand that even after marriage all of us will have to continue to die to our will in some form or another. We should practice becoming unselfish during our season of singleness.

We train for many things in life. Doctors go to college for seven years and then have four years of training. They specialize in different areas of medicine. They pore over countless books and medical journals. They have hands-on experience with highly knowledgeable doctors guiding them along the way.

Teachers train for four years to be able to educate their students. They pore over books and research papers. They spend at least one semester in a real classroom with a seasoned teacher, learning the ropes.

In the same manner that a person's training to become a doctor benefits a patient or a person's training to become a teacher benefits a student, learning to become a godly, selfless person during your single years will bless your mate in ways you cannot imagine. Who would want to marry someone who is selfish and unprepared?

What in Tracy and Mike's friendship primed them to shift their focus away from serving and enjoying God? First, they monopolized each other's time. Even if Mike did not reciprocate with special feelings for Tracy, he spent a major portion of time with someone he never thought would be his wife. Think about the time they spent together, and do the math. Each week has about fifty-six hours of free time outside of eight hours sleep a night and eight hours work a day. Tracy and Mike spent:

• Sunday: 3 hours together (that is, if it did not extend into the afternoon and evening)

• Wednesday: 4 hours together

• Saturday: another 4 hours together at least

That's a total of eleven hours, or about 20 percent of their free time, that Tracy and Mike spent with each other weekly. This does not include calling, e-mailing, and text messaging. Wow! What would you do with eleven spare hours each week?

Many singles in our culture have not been told to take advantage of their primary purpose, which God sanctified for this time in their life. Blessed with this undivided focus, unmarried people have hours available in a week when they could baby-sit for a young couple at no cost, become mentors, make an effort to know families in their church, hit their knees in intercessory prayer, develop a deep accountability with an older man or woman, read their Bibles distraction-free . . . The list could go on and on. What a waste of time, energy, and mental exercise Mike and Tracy spent on each other rather than focusing on God.

"Even as the Son of Man came not to be served but to serve, and to give his life. . . . So you also, when you have done all that you were commanded, say, 'We are unworthy servants; we have only done what was our duty'" (Matt. 20:28; Luke 17:10). Our purpose in life is clear and simple to understand when we look through spiritual glasses rather than cultural glasses. Christ came to serve, and His desire for us is to function likewise during our days, whether we are single or married.

Instead of focusing on serving God, Tracy focused on Mike, their friendship, and a potential future relationship. Mike and Tracy's first error was the precious time spent on a futile relationship.

Spoken for

The second error in their relationship was that they appeared to be a couple to those around them. Tracy was "spoken for" in her mind, and to accept a date with anyone else would have been cheating on Mike. When we have reached the point that we will not even accept a date from someone else because of a guy friend, we know we have gone too far in our minds. We have become wrapped up with the notion that this relationship will progress to the next level. Tracy's heart and mind were occupied with Mike. This led to a blurred reading of God's prompting. At that point no one could come close to her heart.

"Say, what's wrong with two people spending time together? I mean, Mike probably protected her from some other jerk! What others thought was their problem, not Tracy's or Mike's, right?" This may be difficult to explain because it is such a mental battle. Were their hearts pure? Did Tracy spend time with Mike because of the friendship or to continue her illusion that she and Mike might have a future together? Were the intentions of their friendship clear? Did they remain emotionally whole for their mates?

In all of your friendships with members of the opposite sex, can you openly say to each person, "This is where our friendship stands; we are just friends"? If you can't, you need to reconsider the purpose of your friendship and whether your heart is in too deep. This defining of the purpose of your friendship should, ideally, come from the man. Just as Christ is the initiator and humans are the responders, so too is the man the initiator and the woman the responder.

Emotional Attachment

As discussed earlier, the Bible commands women to learn to love their husbands, just as it commands husbands to love their wives. It states,

"Older women . . . are to . . . train the young women to love their husbands and children" (Titus 2:3-4). "Wives, submit to your own husbands, as to the Lord" (Eph. 5:22). During the time of learning to love our husbands, the emotional connection is the glue that holds our marriages together. I believe this is part of the reason a woman stays with a man who abuses her—her emotional connection is so strong, it keeps her there. This emotional attachment creates a devotion that makes some women behave as if they threw common sense out the window.

When a single woman uses this emotional glue to hold together or hold on to her male friendships, it will not have the same adhesiveness when she finally marries. Think about a Post-it note. The first time you use the note, it stays straight, the edges don't curl, and it stays in place almost wherever you put it. After a couple of uses, how well does that Post-it note stick to any surface? Not well at all. It loses even more stickiness when you put it on a dusty surface. The more impure the surface, the less ability it has to fuse. It is the same with the emotions of a woman. The more she sticks to Mr. Wrong, the less available she is to stick to Mr. Right.

Ego Booster

The third error in Tracy and Mike's friendship was that they stroked each other's egos. Tracy paid special attention to Mike. What an ego booster, having a beautiful girl give you undivided attention. And when Mike shared his thoughts, feelings, and struggles with Tracy, she felt emotionally connected. But without a clear definition of their relationship, someone was bound to get hurt.

Whelchel also touches on this issue in her book *Common Mistakes Singles Make*:

> I also observed too often that many singles—yes, Christian singles—
> enjoy sending signals and then disowning them. After all, it's an ego trip
> to think that one or two people are "on your string," hoping you'll come
> their way sooner or later, even if they're not attractive to you.

It is easy for men and women to lose focus during those single years when a man or woman steps into their life, especially if God has not done the prompting. For Tracy and Mike, losing their focus happened without their even realizing it.

Joy in Singleness

We need to become friends with our singleness. The number one goal during this time is to fix ourselves on loving God with all our heart, soul, mind, and strength. When you grow in your love for Him, you will desire to conform yourself to Him. You will put aside your own wishes and start living for His. Being single will then be easier. It may not come overnight, but with prayer and much reading of His holy and pure Word, you will see that His ways are best for you.

This may be one of the biggest mental battles you will have. It takes perseverance and tenacity. You can't give up. You have to fight the good fight of faith. Repent of thinking that marriage will solve your problems. Learn to fall in love with God. Trust Him for everything. He cares about all the details of your life. God has answered so many of my little prayer requests that it's now easier to trust Him with the big things. We like to be our own masters, but God is the Master, and He deserves that respect.

God wants you to have joy in your singleness, and He wants you to know He's not going to keep you single a day longer than He plans. He wants us to use our time as singles to serve and enjoy Him and to focus on obeying and trusting Him. As the old hymn states, "Trust and obey, for there is no other way, to be happy in Jesus, but to trust and obey." So true, so true!

For Guys Only

Your thought life may be a little different than ours. Women are quick to picture themselves married to you in many different ways—wedding dress, kids, family vacations. You may not ponder what her name sounds like next to your last name, but you may indulge in lustful thoughts that are ungodly. "But I say to you that everyone who looks at a woman with lustful intent has already committed adultery with her in his heart" (Matt. 5:28).

Your sex life in marriage may look different than you imagined when you were single, and if you are easily attracted to pornography now, it will not end once you are married. Again, if your thought life is not under submission to God, your lustful thoughts will plague you even after you are married.

Let me explain it in this way. When a woman dresses in alluring clothes, what is your reaction? It could be lust, or it could be an attitude of "please dress modestly so I will not stumble." We women must realize how visual men are, and because of that we should wear modest clothes. Not because we don't have the right to wear what we want, but for the benefit of the spiritual life of our brothers in Christ.

Okay, you men, when you read that Tracy's heart was "taken," you might have thought, "What! How could she get herself that wrapped up in Mike? What's her problem? She must have been really desperate." Again it comes back to the female heart. Here is some more insight on women that may help turn on some light bulbs. No matter how much some may fight it, women are very emotional. "Okay, I definitely knew that!" you say. But it's the God-given ability in women to easily connect on an emotional level with a man that strengthens her marriage, not her male friendships. Did you catch that? This capacity to attach our hearts effortlessly is to be the glue for our marriages, not for our male friendships.

Ask yourselves these questions: What level of devotion do you want from your wife? Do you want your wife to still hold a glimmer of devotion for Jimmy from her high school days? Or do you want to know that your wife saved her heart, all of it, for you and no one else? Remember, a virtuous woman does her husband good *all* the days of her life," not just her married days (Prov. 31:12). When a woman is kept free from any friendship that has emotional devotion, she is saving it all for you! Wow! That's cool stuff.

To explain how deep this connection is, you need to understand that when you ask a girl out for coffee, she could be planning your wedding, naming your kids, and designing your beautiful vacation home. I am not joking. This is really how women think. I have been guilty of this, and the guy had no idea how adorable our kids were and how grand our vacation home would be. Please note that this doesn't necessarily mean the girl is stark-raving desperate. She is just being an emotional woman, the way God created her.

chapter THIRTEEN

Seeing Christ's Design

THE LORD GOD SAID, 'It is not good that the man should be alone; I will make him a helper fit for him'" (Gen. 2:18). I'm sure most of you have heard the joke—probably many times over—that says God created man, saw He could do better, and so created woman. Women usually laugh heartily at the joke, though it is not really funny. Upon deeper inspection of God's Word, and with an awareness of God's basis for creating males and females, we will uncover a better understanding of our purpose and function as unmarried people.

Why did God create marriage? Was it for friendship, companionship, love, to populate the earth? Or was it so He could watch us struggle with not having something we want? What was Adam doing before Eve? Why did God institute marriage, and why should the path toward marriage maintain consistency with His plan?

Adam and Eve

God created man and saw that he did not have a suitable helpmate. Adam was keeping busy in the garden, working and enjoying fellowship with *Elohim* (the Creator Lord). He was just minding his own business, naming the animals (Gen. 2:19), and having uninterrupted communion with God. Then one day God said, "It is not good that the man should be alone." God saw that Adam needed a counterpart or helper, and this person was to be a blessing in his life. Wow! God created a person especially for Adam, one who would be one flesh with him and would fit his needs.

In *The Power of Femininity: Rediscovering the Art of Being a Woman*, Michelle McKinney Hammond puts it bluntly:

> God had a brilliant idea! . . . Poor thing, this creature needed help. God had given him a lot of work to do, and He realized that Adam needed help staying focused on it. He would need extra encouragement from time to time. He needed someone to fill in the blanks, take up the slack, and keep him together. He needed a "helpmate," a partner—someone designed especially to complement him in every way. This person would add dimension to his life, would be strong where he was weak. This person, called woman, would assist him in completing his assignment to subdue, maintain order, cultivate and take care of God's creation, and to be fruitful and multiply. These things he could not do without her help.

I often find it amazing that Adam had such a beautiful, *distraction-free* relationship with God, and yet God found it "good" for a woman to be his companion. God created woman to be a helper for man. Some women may have their noses bent out of shape when the Bible says they were created for man. But after God stated, "It is not good that the man should be alone," He made "a helper fit for him." Paul reinforced this wonderful purpose for women in 1 Corinthians 11:8-9: "For man was not made from woman, but woman from man. Neither was man created for the woman, but woman for man."

Fortified with this knowledge, we women should feel honored to be qualified for such an important position. Men need us! While sitting in a large medical recliner, I was telling my dentist about my book project—I was in the middle of writing a book on singles. Since he's been married for more than thirty-five years, I decided to ask for his opinion on being single. He answered laughingly, "Don't get married." Then just as quickly he added, "No, we men need you women."

Helpmate

Since women were created to be helpers for men, why does the desire for marriage surprise women? Why does the desire for a home of our own shock us? Why does it anger others? Why do others deny or suppress it? We have lost sight of the beautiful role a woman plays in a man's life. God created us to serve and work alongside a man. This natural, God-given longing is to be treasured; yet many of us perceive it as a burden we must bear. Some say that our "equal rights" are not being respected. But we must look at everything through God's perspective, not according to what the world is telling us.

Desiring to be a wife or a husband is what God has put in the hearts of many of His children. He longs to reveal Himself through our marriages. However, when we allow our own selfish desires to take root, His goodness and mercies cannot shine through. Adam and Eve were put together to demonstrate Christ's lordship and the church's submission.

In His boundless love and grace, God longs for us to know His love for us, to know the sacrifices He was willing to make so that one day we might be with Him forever. He knows us well. He created us. He knows we are programmed to understand word pictures. Think about all the prophets, the parables, and His own Son's death on the cross—they all paint pictures of God's heart. God is the most attractive, most powerful being; yet He made Himself invisible so we would follow Him based not on looks or riches but on love. He uses the daily rotation of the earth to illustrate the idea of His new mercies each morning. Snow is used in the Bible to represent the whiteness of our sins when we have been washed with Jesus' blood (Isa. 1:18).

Hosea presents one of the most well-defined word pictures in the Bible. God asked Hosea to marry a prostitute to show Israel's unfaithfulness and God's enduring love. Time and time again God asked Hosea to take his unfaithful wife back, and time and time again Hosea obeyed God (read the story in Hosea 1–3). This portrays God's relationship with His children—He continually forgives us, calls us back to Himself, and loves us.

A Mirror

God created marriage to mirror our relationship with Him and the love He has for us. The church is the bride, and Jesus is the Bridegroom. In the book of Revelation, John uses this analogy (19:7; 21:9). The marriage will take place, and the bride (the church) must prepare herself for the Bridegroom.

The Lord longs for earthly marriages to point people to Him. He wants the glory He deserves. When you are considering marriage, certain questions must be asked: Will this marriage point people to the Father? Will this marriage honor Him above all else? This is His reason for marriage. He created marriage to show His perfect love. When two believers marry, they must lay aside selfish desires and know that God will use the love they have for each other to show others the love of the Father. This is an awesome responsibility and should not be taken with even a hint of selfishness. A marriage of two believers should be so drastically different than that of two nonbelievers that the world should crave what we have—God's love. Marriage is one of God's evangelistic tools.

Before Christ

When we think about our pre-Christ life, we can see the dramatic difference His love has made. Many of you laid aside old sinful behaviors and became new creatures in Him. If you think about it, your commitment to Christ was made with little knowledge of what was to come, right? You may look back and think, "How did I get here?" The trials and pain, joy and excitement are all part of getting to know God, but did you know that when you started? Most of us who know the Lord could never have imagined what our loving God would do for us. The same is true for marriage.

The beginning of Tracy and Mike's relationship could have been the beginning of a household in which Mike would be the leader. Therefore he needed to step up to the plate and should have clearly explained his intentions to Tracy. Just as Christ is the initiator, the man should initiate a relationship. If Mike did not know his intentions, then he should have backed off and let God show him what his future was to be, with or without Tracy. When does the responsibility of the household begin? With a wedding ring? With an engagement ring? Or at the beginning of a relationship?

God's Picture

After an engagement followed by a marriage ceremony, the picture God is painting with a husband and wife becomes clearer. We see that the husband is to protect, lead, serve, and provide for the wife. The wife is to submit, obey, and follow the guidance of her husband. When each partner lays aside personal will and replaces it with the mate's wishes, a beautiful thing takes place. I am not even sure there are words to fully express this. The husband is free to bear his responsibilities, and the wife is free to provide a loving environment.

I would like to point out that I am speaking of the norm. Most people would say, "But what about this or that situation?" Well, God calls a husband to be a servant leader and a wife to submit regardless of what someone's mate is doing.

We must guard our hearts, keeping them pure for our future bride-groom or bride. God is the Creator of marriage, and He desires marriage to be used to honor Him. He longs for us to understand, through the path to marriage and in marriage itself, our relationship with Christ.

chapter FOURTEEN

Preparing for Marriage

THERE IS FREEDOM IN SAVING your emotions for your spouse and spending time in your single years in God's private classroom. With God's way, you protect emotions that are to be freely given to the mate of His choice for you.

Some of you—chances are, many of you—have been in an undefined emotional relationship. Most people have had a couple of these risky interactions. Let's look at some things to do that may help heal some of your battle wounds. We will examine things you can do while you are waiting on God to reveal His will in your daily life and in your future.

First, there's no easy cure for the wounded heart when it comes to healing from an emotional relationship. Time may be all you have. It sounds so cliché, but time will aid in mending your broken heart. Time has been the biggest factor in repairing my heart from undefined emotional relationships.

Second, you need to avoid spending any more emotions that should be saved. Assess your current relationships. Are they defined? Do you know whether you are future mates or just friends? Back away emotionally from any undefined relationship or work toward defining it.

Backing Off

Backing off may be incredibly hard because your heart will tell you that backing away from this friendship is illogical. "I mean, this person is still my brother in Christ, right? How could I be rude to him?" you may ask. But if this "rudeness" is protection, then it is not rudeness—it is guarding your heart. And God tells you to guard your heart: "Above all else, guard your heart, for it is the wellspring of life" (Prov. 4:23, NIV). If you don't guard your heart, wellsprings may come pouring from your teary eyes, not from your heart.

Let's look at the current culturally accepted way of building relationships. You get to know someone—he doesn't like you the way you like him—heart pain results. Or you meet someone new—you get to know him (a little more guarded this time)—you don't really like him the way he likes you—you break his heart. Or perhaps you meet another potential mate—you get to know him (even more guarded, maybe a little cynical)—you both like each other—you get physically intimate—you break up. Or you meet yet another person—you stay really guarded emotionally—you know in your heart that this is God's mate for you, but the chance of heart pain is too great to risk the commitment. My suggestion for guarding your heart ends the cycle and doesn't sound so bad after all.

Nathaniel and Andrew Ryun state this clearly in their book *It's a Lifestyle: Discipleship in Our Relationships*:

> Emotions are given away, hearts tied together, and then torn apart. Emotions and feelings are trampled with impunity. . . . This continual giving of emotions, and then separating, leaves wounds that can last for years and prove a tough obstacle to overcome in marriage. The "hearts" given away in marriage are not much more than bruised illusions of healthy and whole hearts.

If you decide that stepping away from a relationship is God's best for your heart and emotions, then it will be a call to wholehearted obedience. When I struggled in an undefined emotional relationship, I fasted from the guy. What do I mean by "fasted from" him? Well, I stopped seeing him, which was hard because we lived on the same campus. I did not go out of my way to talk to him. I did not manipulate situations to see him. I basically avoided him. You know what he did? Nothing. It did not even faze him. This was a big clue for me. Fasting from him was one of the smartest things I did. I thank God for His insight. Though it did not cure me of having feelings for the guy, it did put our relationship into perspective.

Defining and Dealing

Another thing you can do is define your relationship. Be bold enough to ask politely where you stand. What are his intentions? Don't be afraid of ending your fantasy. Whenever you think about or are with that person, you are wasting time you could spend finding and developing a relationship with your future mate. Your future mate may be watching you and thinks you're dating someone else.

Dealing with relationship baggage will look different for each of you. Pray that God will show you what He wants you to do. Dealing with any baggage before you walk down the aisle will enhance the success of your marriage. If relational rubbish is not dealt with before the "I do's," one or both partners may be so into self-gratification that the marriage will not be honoring to God or focused on Him.

Let's remember that contentment is not the gift of celibacy, nor is it the magic key that gives God the go-ahead to send a spouse your way. Being content also does not mean giving up hope. Once you have come to a place where you are content with God's plan for your life and you strive to have an undistracted devotion to Him, how do you enroll in God's classroom?

Enrollment in God's Classroom

First, continue to seek Him with all you have. This is a *moment-by-moment* choice you must make. It requires dying to your will—dying to what you want and replacing it with what God wants. This is the hardest part of obedience. Our wills are stubborn, and we have become good at avoiding the act of allowing our hearts to be molded into the image of Christ. Who are we to decide what to allow God to change or not to change?

Second, you want to make sure you are serving God. This will look different for each one of us. Look at the time that you have, and ask the Lord to show where you need to serve.

One mistake to avoid when looking to serve is trying to minister where you are not called. Keeping yourself busy with lots of ministries will not satisfy, but serving where He wants you is tremendously rewarding. When you are seeking Him first, He can do awesome things and open doors of ministry you thought were impossible.

Third, become emotionally unavailable to the opposite sex. Do I mean buy a wedding ring and pretend you are married? Of course not! I mean keep yourself away from situations in which your heart can be drawn to a person and possibly take your focus off the Lord. Have you ever thought about how God feels when you give attention, time, thoughts, and emotions to another human and not to Him? "For your Maker is your husband" (Isa. 54:5a). If you saw God as your mate, how jealous would He be over you?

Thinking of God as our spouse seems to put some things into perspective. When we pray from the selfishness of our hearts, we are telling God that He's not enough. He wants to be all we desire; so *that* should be our prayer. We must have pure motives when we go to God with the request of a mate. It pleases God to satisfy us when our hearts, motives, and actions are pure. "You ask and do not receive, because you ask wrongly, to spend it on your passions" (Jas. 4:3). As I look back over my journals, I see times that I placed myself in situations where I could easily be emotionally intimate with men. I would pray with them, spend one-on-one time with them, tell them my pains, and share dreams and hopes with them. My heart was deceiving me. I thought I could be around them and not step over the line of emotional and spiritual intimacy, but I couldn't. My heart was left unprotected.

As I said earlier, my heart has bumps and bruises on it, and my desire is to see others learn from some of my mistakes. God revealed something big to me about the time I would spend with single guys. One guy with whom I shared a deep emotional connection got married a few years ago. When I found out he was getting married, the thought came to me, *Every time we were alone, praying, talking, sharing, and laughing, his future wife and my future husband were sitting right between us.*

Whoa! God hit me over the head with that one! I looked back and saw how conversations and actions would have been completely avoided had this been our mind-set.

Personally, I have learned to not place myself in situations where my heart might be drawn to an unmarried man. I have a tendency to start imagining things that are not there, and before I know it—of course, this can take all of two minutes—my mind is off in the La-la Land of Marriage. Can this be difficult to avoid? Yes! Does avoiding it go completely against the flow of the world? Yes! Does God sustain us? Yes!

Fourth, ask God to enroll you in His "Wife Training Program." The Holy Spirit is our teacher. If you know deep in your heart that your desire to be married is from the Lord, then ask Him to prepare you.

We go to college for four years or more to prepare for a profession. Yet most people do not prepare for the life role that will influence generations to come. Mull over in your mind the fact that when you enter into a marriage you are, Lord willing, going to create a child—an *eternal* being. How much time have you put into preparing to guide, lead, and develop that child for the kingdom of God? Your children (whether born to you or adopted) are the only things you can take to heaven with you. That, in and of itself, is powerful and should not be taken lightly.

Preparing for Marriage

Preparing to be married will look different for men and for women. Our role as wives will affect generations to come. We have lost sight of how influential God created women to be. When we strive to obtain power over a man, we leave no room for the man to be a man, and thus we lose our ability to influence. We feel frustrated and hurt. There are some things that I have learned to do in order to prepare to be a wife. It is not easy! This goes against human nature, and only through God's goodness can we ever learn these things.

Pray

Pray for your husband now. A wife who prays for her husband is a powerful tool for the kingdom of heaven. As for me, I have been faithfully praying for my husband since 1996. Each year has a different focus, and it will be awesome to see God bring those prayer requests to completion when He chooses.

Submit

Learn submission. In our flesh we women are leaders willing to take on whatever conflicts are necessary to mend a situation. (Again I am speaking in general terms.) When we submit and follow, we are doing so through the grace of God. Coming under the authority of a man is not easy for most women. We live in a culture that tells us this type of submission is irrational and ludicrous, but Scripture sees it differently. "I want you to understand that the head of every man is Christ, the head of a wife is her husband, and the head of Christ is God" (1 Cor. 11:3).

Women and men misunderstand submission. Because of this common misunderstanding, we women tend to put up our defenses and let our independent spirits take over. We can be feisty, and that quality can be used for a greater good or can tear a family apart. "The wisest of women builds her house, but folly with her own hands tears it down" (Prov. 14:1).

When we as women truly understand submission, our lives will flow at a much smoother pace. Often we do not submit because we feel the process is taking a bit too long. This is the number one reason I struggle with submitting to my father. I make decisions much faster than he does. Does that mean my decisions are better than his? No. For whatever reasons, I am called to submit to my father and to my husband, at their pace, giving them space to allow the Holy Spirit to work.

Also, when we submit and allow a husband to lead in a godly fashion, we obey the order God has established. God's order of authority is God, man, woman. So when we come under the authority of a husband, we are under God's authority. Men like to be appreciated and respected. Ephesians 5:33 states, "Let the wife see that she respects her husband." Respecting your husband will include honoring his decisions and his timing. It also allows him the freedom to trust that you will not lose heart when he has to take a step of faith in areas in your marriage and life. With the support of a wife, a man can be successful. As has been often said, "Behind every good man is a good woman." When respect and submission are channeled in a godly way, men are freed to be servant leaders in all areas of their lives.

Submitting does not include manipulation. We become very good at manipulating situations to obtain what we want. This can be dangerous because no matter what the outcome, true satisfaction will not occur. We have a great deal of influence over men, and that must be kept in God's will and not used for selfish gain.

Learning to submit before the "I do's" will greatly lessen the pain of learning submission after marriage.

Protect

Once you are married, let your husband protect your emotions so you are free to be the love-giver of the family. This emotional tenderness that God gave women is to be used to provide an atmosphere in our homes that is warm and inviting. When we don't let a husband protect our emotions, we have less emotion to give to him and our children. The way I see it, we are to be the love-makers in the family, creating a home that our husband will want to come to after work, not a place filled with battles, disorder, and headaches.

As we discussed earlier, men have egos and do not like conflict when the outcome is unknown. As wives, we must learn to provide an environment in which a husband is free to speak without ramifications. I have seen men keep their mouths shut at meetings or social groups because of what their wives may say on the drive home. You know what I am talking about here. What husband wants the "wait until we get home and you'll get it" attitude? No man I know feels free to express himself with that type of wife.

Learning to be protected goes against everything in us. We have Eve tendencies in our flesh—being told one thing that would protect us and doing the opposite. However, protection is becoming to a woman of any age. Ask God to teach you what protection looks like during your unmarried years. Again, this is the line of authority that God set up!

Prepare

Prepare your home. For many of my single years I lived at home with my parents; so most of the items I used belong to them. But I began my own collection. Ever heard the term *hope chest*? I think the idea of a hope chest is a wonderful thing. I expect to enter into a marriage with basic items already purchased. Being ready to set up a home will prepare you for the mental and emotional changes that will take place within the first years of marriage.

I explained to a married girlfriend how I felt it was important for me to prepare tangibly for marriage. Over the phone I could almost feel her look of, "Huh?" Then she sweetly asked, "Well, Heather, are you dating anyone?"

"No," I replied, feeling somewhat stupid. Then the conversation carried on to other things. She and her husband had longed for a child, but God had not blessed them with a baby. Within two weeks they adopted a little boy. She told me how chaotic her house was upon the arrival of their son. Then a light bulb went off in my head. I said, "That is why I am preparing for marriage. Most people have nine months to prepare for a child, but I don't know how long I'll have to prepare for my marriage. So I am getting ready. I want to step smoothly into my marriage." Thinking she had plenty of time to prepare for a baby, my friend had an *aha!* moment!

Preparing your home may go beyond buying tangible items. It could include mentally preparing what type of home you want. Not necessarily the style, like country or Victorian, but how you want people to *feel* when they walk into your home. My parents had a vision when they built the house they currently live in. Part of that vision was to construct a home that is warm, inviting, and cozy. I believe they succeeded. Most people say that when they hit the first step to my parents' country-style, wrap-around porch they feel like they are coming home. Create a vision for your home. How do you want it to function? Do you want it to be a place of rest and comfort? What will aid you in creating this vision?

Being able to have a smooth transition into marriage—emotionally, spiritually, and physically—will provide a calm, peaceful life. Again, preparing oneself for marriage will be a blessing for both parties.

Stop

As single women, we need to stop treating men as if they are our husbands. We are created with a nature that longs to serve and please a man, but when we do this, we take away *his* desire for a wife. I have seen single girls fuss over who is going to serve a guy his coffee. Really, let him get it himself if your motives are not pure. Let's not misuse serving to satisfy a longing for a husband. Also, if women are giving men companionship outside of marriage, he will never hunger for female companionship inside marriage. Women have the ability to create a void in a man's life so he will become self-motivated to fill it with the presence of a wife. It's a new twist on the old saying, "playing hard to get."

Recap

Women, does your flirtatious attitude make you ready to settle down with one man? When you open up emotionally with a man, are you giving away emotions that should be saved for your future mate? Are you learning now what it means to be submissive and to have a quiet and gentle spirit? Can you effectively and smoothly run a house and make it a haven of peace and love?

How much time have you wasted thus far? When you are in your single years, you must realize that most likely you will one day have a family. You must make decisions today that will positively affect them later.

Men and women need to search Scripture and ask God to show them what qualities He wants in a godly husband or wife. For me personally, God has shown me what a quiet and gentle spirit looks like. When I think of someone with such a spirit, I envision someone who is able to take whatever life tosses her way with peace and joy. She doesn't seek to serve her own needs. She has power perfectly blended with seasoned self-control.

If you are not preparing yourself for marriage, you can experience frustration when expectations are not met. I have seen newly married men who do not protect their wives because they feel suffocated by the new commitment. I see new brides who flirt with other guys and have a hard time communicating with their new husbands. This is shameful.

When you walk down the aisle, do you want a groom who does not know what it means to protect and provide for his bride? Do you want to be stubborn and independent? The time is now, while you are single, to learn how to be what God wants you to be.

Let God train you. If that means He brings older adults or your parents into your life, then submit to Him by accepting His provision. He knows what is best. During this season of singleness, present yourself as a living sacrifice, and wait on your holy Father. This is pleasing in His sight.

Remaining fixed on God's plan and His friendship during these years will save you and your future mate a great deal of pain. God's ways are far better than anything you could do on your own!

For Guys Only

Although I am a woman, God has given me some understanding about the roles of a husband. Consider the following:

1. *Start praying for your wife and family.* Your prayers as a husband will greatly affect how you treat your wife (1 Pet. 3:7). Covering your wife and family in prayer now will bring a great harvest later. You will reap the benefits or consequences of what you sow.

2. *Practice being a leader.* Most men, in the flesh, are followers. (I am speaking in general terms.) They would rather go with the flow and follow a leader. As a husband, you are required by God to lead your family (Eph. 5:23). And when you lead your family, God receives the glory because in your flesh you desire to follow. Therefore, you are leading in your weakness. This in turn glorifies God. "[God] said to me, 'My grace is sufficient for you, for my power is made perfect in weakness.' Therefore I will boast all the more gladly of my weaknesses, so that the power of Christ may rest upon me" (2 Cor. 12:9). God not only asks you to lead but to be a servant leader, just as Christ is to the church. Serving your mom, sisters, and brothers will help you gain a better understanding of what this service is to look like. I would recommend that you do not try to learn to be a leader with a godly sister in Christ unless your relationship is clearly defined. To a woman, this can be confusing. But God can show you areas in which to lead before you are married that will benefit your future wife and family.

3. *Ask God to teach you what it means to protect your wife and family.* This refers to protection not only from the elements and harmful situations but also protection of your wife's heart. A woman has a sensitive heart. Her emotions and feelings are to be sheltered from the elements of

the world. This means that you, as the man, will have to stick your neck out and be willing to accept success or failure.

An example of this protection came during a girlfriend's engagement stage. I took time to prod her with questions. One question was whether she planned on working after they had kids. She said she didn't know if she would or not, but either way her soon-to-be husband was behind her decision 100 percent. Some may say, "What a supportive husband." I say, "He's not supportive at all." Down the road let's say my friend chooses to work, and she is completely stressed out. What is her husband's responsibility in the matter? None! His out? "Well, it was your choice to work." Therefore, he is not taking on the success or failure of her working. His ego is protected, but his wife's heart is not.

As a woman, I desire my husband to protect me emotionally so that I have more love to bestow upon him. This is a beautiful thing. A man's ability to protect his wife in all areas will greatly enhance the quality of their marriage.

4. Prepare your home. How I would love to marry a man who has been saving money for marriage. When a single guy spends money foolishly, he is taking away money from his future wife and family. Most of you will have a family; you just don't have it now. My friend Bob saved money for his wife and family beginning when he was seven. When he approached marriage he had money to buy a nice ring, pay for their honeymoon, and still have money for a down payment on a condo. He thought ahead and did not live for the moment.

Adapting these few points for your life will better equip you to be a godly husband and a man who has his heart directly hooked up to the heart of the Father.

Let's recap. Gentlemen, are you being prepared to take responsibility for a wife and a family by the lifestyle you are living now? Are you learning what it means to protect and provide for your wife? Does a carefree lifestyle prepare you to be a godly husband?

chapter FIFTEEN

Dating Done Differently

MY FAITH IS COMPLETELY RESTING on God to provide a husband for me. I trust that He is preparing a mate for me and me for a mate. It is my faith that casts away any doubt. I have asked God for certain qualities in a husband, and I have to be patient while God works on my mate's heart. When these qualities are answered, I will know beyond a shadow of a doubt this is the right man for me. Do I think God is someday going to say, "Oh no, I forgot to introduce Heather to her husband! I guess she will be single the rest of her life"? Hardly. I know I will not remain single a day longer than God wants me to be.

Before I get practical, I would ask you to remove any preconceived ideas you have about the Christian dating scene or even what you think I am telling you. Read carefully. This is what I believe God has called me to do. You need to be pure, and that may take a different shape for you than for me. The Jews had their own preconceived idea of the Messiah, and when He came they did not recognize Him. Try your best not to limit God.

Accountability

The first part of this alternative dating is to have the total involvement of your family in your process toward marriage. My sisters hold me accountable and help me avoid the pitfalls of premature emotional intimacy. Having true accountability is key in maintaining emotional purity.

My parents give me guidance and advice, along with protecting my heart. My parents have my heart (Proverbs 23:26 states that God wants us to give our parents our hearts), and I trust them with it. I have turned my heart to my father, and he has turned his heart to me. Malachi 4:6 states that through His prophet God would "turn the hearts of fathers to their children and the hearts of children to their fathers." My mother and father have loved me from before I was born and have cared for me more than any other human beings. I know that I will seek my father's advice and guidance along the path toward marriage. I cherish his advice. Does that mean he is a control freak and wants to dictate everything I do? No. He sees my heart, and just like my Heavenly Father, he wants what is best for me.

Unfortunately, I believe that many women have not experienced a man in their life who had their best interests at heart. So for them this type of submission is hard to understand. So many people have been hurt and abused that this level of trust seems nearly impossible, but nothing is too difficult for God. He can heal and restore your heart in ways no one can even fathom. My prayer for anyone who doesn't have a solid relationship with her father is either that she will be able to repair that relationship or find an older Christian couple to help in this process. Having the guidance of others will help you avoid intimacy before a commitment.

Blessing

Since intimacy and commitment go hand in hand, when the man I am to marry comes along, God already will have been preparing him for me. I pray we will get to know each other around our families and friends. As I said, I rarely spend extended one-on-one time with any man; so to know me, my future husband will have to learn about me around other people. Also, I have asked God to work a miracle in the situation. He can protect me from becoming emotional before the time He ordains it. I pray that God will give me wisdom in making this choice, and I know He has put people in my path to help me along.

I have made a conscious choice to seek my parents' advice and counsel as I move into a relationship. I trust my parents. Many of you have broken relationships with your parents. If you do not have a relationship of trust with your parents, then I encourage you to pray that God will repair damaged relationships with your parents or bring into your life some older, wiser Christians who desire to guide you. Seek advice from people you trust, and allow yourself to really listen to their advice and assistance.

An older friend and I talked about this issue. She was not raised in a Christian home; so looking to her mother and stepfather for guidance was a ridiculous thought when she was younger. Through studying the Word and hearing godly advice, she decided that her decision to give up a well-established career at age twenty-nine in order to attend Bible college needed the blessing of her stepfather, a nonbeliever.

God arranged their meeting time perfectly, and she laid her plans before him. She had purposed in her heart that whatever he said she would obey. After explaining the pros and cons, her heart behind the matter, and her plans, she waited for her stepfather's answer. "That sounds like a good idea. Your career will be waiting for you when you are done," he responded. She had his blessing.

As she looks over this pivotal event in her life, she sees how God showed her that whether or not her stepfather was a believer, she was still to honor him. At Bible college she met her future husband, and today their marriage is truly a picture of Christ and His church.

God Is in Control

God asks us to take a leap of faith by giving up our full control in finding a mate. God can do anything He wants. He is rich, powerful, well networked, and ready to bless His obedient children. Who wouldn't want Him to find her a mate? I mean, can you imagine how big His "little black book" is? He's the ultimate dating service!

God has set up roles when it comes to the steps we take toward marriage. Proverbs 18:22 says, "He who *finds* a wife finds a good thing and obtains favor from the LORD" (italics mine). So the way I see it, I am to be found, not to be out looking myself. Whenever someone asked my sister where she was going to find her husband, she always responded, "Is he lost?"

The man's role is going to be different. "He who finds a wife . . ." The man is to do the finding and the initiating. My prayer is that any man looking for a wife would be willing to come under the guidance of his father or an older Christian man. Again, Christ is the example a man is to follow. Christ is the initiator, not the church. When women are aggressive, they leave no room for the man to be the initiator, which sets a tone for the relationship.

Christian Brothers

Paul wrote some wonderful advice to Timothy (a young man) on how to treat younger women—"like sisters, in all purity" (1 Tim. 5:2). The Greek word translated "all" is *pas*, meaning all things individually and in their totality. A man must treat a younger woman like a sister and "in all purity." How does a brother treat his sister? I do not have any brothers, but I know that in most family situations brothers and sisters do not pay attention to one over the other, communicating feelings of "you're special," nor do they step over any lines of physical intimacy. They also generally have no hidden agendas; where they stand with each other is clear. Do brothers and sisters know one another? Yes. Do they care for one another? Yes. So what is Paul talking about? Paul stated that all women with whom a man comes in contact must be treated with "all purity." Only God can give the green light to take a relationship to another level of intimacy. And when God gives the green light, purity remains in its proper place.

Some of you may say Mike treated Tracy as a sister, but did he really? He set her apart, made her feel special, and without even knowing it took over her thought life. In a physical sense he did treat her purely, but what about her emotions? He was not up-front with his intentions. If he had been, she might not have become so taken with him. Now Tracy allowed herself to become worked up over Mike, so we cannot put all the blame on him. She could have asked him to define their friendship. They had closeness but no commitment. He was taking away emotions that should have been saved for her husband.

Since the husband is the head of the wife, he is responsible for sticking his neck out and being held accountable. When an unmarried man sticks his neck out with a young lady, he is preparing himself for the role God has assigned to him in marriage. Christ put His life on the line, with no guarantee that we would respond. What a great life lesson men can learn in taking the initiative in relationships.

Involvement

As I and a man move on to another level of getting to know each other, I will continue to seek guidance and advice. I see no need in doing this all on my own. After all, God put my parents in my life to help and care for me. I will want the young man to pass my "dad test." My desire is to know that my father thinks highly of the young man I have my eyes on. This safety net will again help me avoid falling in love too quickly.

Since we will spend a great deal of time with other people during the "getting to know you" phase, we will not be as prone to share and discuss things that should be kept private or saved for a more committed relationship. When other people are present, conversation is not allowed to flow in whatever direction it chooses. We will both be protected emotionally from levels of relationship that should come only after a mutual commitment. This does not mean that my family or friends are going to listen to every phone call or screen every e-mail, but it does mean that my heart is protected and I do not have to allow my heart to be devoured or hurt. There is freedom in all of this, and I pray that you will not see this as legalistic.

An example of my dad's involvement came in January 1999. I was an emcee at a Christian conference. A group of women wanted a top-ten list I had written. I asked if they had an e-mail address. They did not, but a man in their group did. They sent this young, single guy my way, and we exchanged e-mail addresses. Later that week I e-mailed him the list.

Several nights later I was online, and he instant-messaged me. We chatted for a while. I told my dad that he seemed nice, and I asked Dad to check him out. Dad sent him an e-mail asking him about his intentions toward me. Surprisingly, the guy was very grateful and thanked my dad for the up-front nature of his e-mail and stated that he had a girlfriend.

Thus I was protected from offering any emotions without a commitment. What if we had kept writing each other and became friends through e-mail? Knowing me, I would have become emotionally entangled with him, thinking maybe this is "the one," only to find out he had a girlfriend.

This saved me from doing any of that. Being free to save those emotions is wonderful, or as Martha Stewart would say, "It's a good thing!"

Does this sound a little crazy? Maybe, but I am thankful I saved myself—and him for that matter—any further hurt. Knowing I have this protective covering over me allows me to serve and focus on God and Him alone.

Protecting

I have an important role as well in protecting my heart. A woman cannot blame it all on a guy if she became emotionally tangled with him. She must look at her own motives and ask if she did anything to create the problem.

For me, I had to rearrange my own thinking when it came to how I spent time with my guy friends. If needed, I would put up a protective fence around my heart. Sometimes it was tangible, like having a girlfriend join a man and me on an activity. Sometimes it was intangible, like a mind-set I needed to put in place as I spent time with a male friend. The biggest thing for me was to not allow my mind to wander too far off reality. This helped protect me from endless ramblings in my journal about my next guy friend.

Again, this process may look different for you. You will need to establish your own set of boundaries for your heart. You know what you can handle. A couple may be out alone and have completely pure hearts; another couple could have impure motives while in a large group of people. The way the Spirit leads will take different forms for each of us. How that manifests itself is between you and the Lord.

Scott and Anne

Emotional purity will take many forms, and the stories below are all ways that my friends' personal purity played out.

First are Scott and Anne. Their first meeting occurred overseas during an extended mission trip. They were still young and were not looking for mates. They were just acquaintances at the time and had mutual friends. It wasn't until a few years later that their friendship was rekindled when Scott worked with Anne's brother-in-law. Anne then had the chance to get to know Scott around her family. She was attracted to his godliness, personality, and character.

Unknown to each other, the Lord began to draw their hearts together as He placed them in circumstances and situations. Neither one let the other know what feelings were there.

When Scott realized he wanted to pursue a relationship with marriage in mind, he talked to Anne's father. Anne's father and Scott spent time in an "interviewing" process, and Scott shared his intentions toward Anne and what God had done in his heart to draw him to her. Anne's father gave Scott permission to then share his heart with Anne and see what God would do.

Because of what God had done in Anne's heart, it didn't take too long for the two of them to know this was God's will for them. They spent time together, getting to know each other on a more intimate level. Many questions were asked and answered, and time was spent with each other's families and friends. God confirmed during this time that they were meant for each other. Ten months later they were married.

Sam and Pam

The next couple is Sam and Pam. When Pam was twelve, her father died. Pam's mother disengaged from her, expecting her to live and think with complete independence as a young adult. Her mom even withheld advice when Pam dared to request it. As a college senior Pam unwisely dated a man who eventually brought an enormous amount of stress, turmoil, and pain into her life. It was the severe trial of that dating relationship that led her to realize how little wisdom she had. She fervently prayed that no other man would pursue her until she had experienced an incredible growth in wisdom. Six years passed.

At Pam's church, which had no singles ministry, she became acquainted with Sam under no pretense of being attracted to him. For more than a year they interacted the same way any members of their friendly church would—no romantic ties and not even a hint of flirtation. So when Sam expressed an interest in Pam, she did not believe him initially. Because he was a few years younger than she, she did not think he was ready for a permanent relationship. She asked Sam to seek counseling from their pastor before she felt at peace with his pursuit. Sam followed through with her request, much to Pam's surprise, and came under the account-ability of their pastor in order to date Pam. Six months later they became engaged. Throughout most of their engagement they met with their pastor weekly. After fourteen years of marriage, Sam and Pam still reap the benefits of their pastor's protection and involvement.

As we see from both of these stories, once the commitment is made to pursue the relationship with marriage in mind, the emotional ties begin. Do you have a better sense of how emotional purity can look for you? Both of these couples remained emotionally pure, and both have such different stories.

Emotionally Pure

Remaining emotionally pure for my mate is exciting. I can't wait to be not only physically pure for him but also emotionally pure. I have faith that these protective measures I am taking will enhance my marriage. Purity is beautiful. Holiness should be desired. The blessings that come from striving toward purity and holiness do not compare to short-term gratification.

In an e-mail I received recently, a woman told me of her desire and struggle to remain emotionally pure.

A friend of mine introduced me to a young man a couple of months ago. We got together a couple times at school in group settings, and then he started calling me. We IM once in a while (he lives in Philly—about thirty minutes from my home in New Jersey). My parents invited him and he came to one of our family nights a few weeks ago. Anyway, the more I get to know him, the more good and godly qualities I see in him. He initiated a relationship-defining conversation a few weeks ago in which we concluded that we are just friends for right now. We are both enjoying getting to know each other, but he is not ready for anything more than friendship right now (he will be a junior in college and I am a fifth-year senior). I was very pleased that he initiated that conversation, and am also pleased about his feelings right now.

I have always prayed that any marriage relationship would begin with a friendship. However, for several reasons it is extremely hard for me to see him just as a friend. I have never really had a male friend, so I am a little unsure of what is proper to share and what is not. Because we were introduced to each other for the purpose of being set up, it's hard to leave behind that idea. Also, I have had such a strong desire for marriage and family for so many years that it's difficult not to get my hopes up. I am desperately seeking the Lord's help and guidance to keep my mind and emotions pure, but this is very hard for me. If it is the Lord's will, I so want my first "dating/courting" experience to be with the man I will marry. I am very concerned about saving my all for him.

This dating alternative isn't easy or a quick fix. It takes time, but it is worth the numerous blessings that come from it.

Another blessing from this dating alternative is that you will know your marriage was not based on you using *anything* to attract a young man's attention. You will always know that he initiated the relationship, and the respect that comes from that is irreplaceable. He will be sure that you responded unconditionally to his initiating. There will never be the "does he like me?" uncertainty. There will be no silly questioning of your intentions with each other. You will never have to turn to the daisy: "He loves me . . . he loves me not." In the long run this will lay a foundation of trust and respect in your marriage. Who could ask for anything more wonderful?

If you feel completely insensitive in this matter of male/female relationships, ask God to pull away some of those calloused layers and make you tender to the boundaries He would have for you.

> *I will give you a new heart, and a new spirit I will put within you. And I will remove the heart of stone from your flesh and give you a heart of flesh. And I will put my Spirit within you, and cause you to walk in my statutes and be careful to obey my rules. (Ezek. 36:26-27)*

When I worked in a ministry in Denver, I signed a contract agreeing that I would not watch R-rated movies for one year. You know what happened? I became very sensitive to the content of movies, even to the point that most PG-13 movies are shocking and undesirable to me. I became resensitized to what is pure, lovely, and of good repute.

When our hearts and motives are pure, our actions will manifest themselves in that direction. As you seek God, serve Him, and focus on Him, He will do awesome things!

After Marriage

Even after marriage we need to continue to strive for purity. Unfortunately, husbands and wives are committing emotional defrauding and emotional fornication with other people at work, at church, and even more so on the Internet. In doing research for this chapter I found hundreds of postings from husbands and wives who discovered that their mates were a little too intimate with someone via the computer. When this problem struck close to home, I began to see the magnitude of this issue.

This is a factual account of Nathan and Darla, long-time family friends. This story perfectly illustrates the gravity of emotional defrauding.

Nineteen years ago this couple married after dating in high school. They attended church regularly, and after eight years of trying unsuccessfully to have children of their own they adopted two children. Darla was a stay-at-home mom and homeschooled the kids. Nathan was a hardworking provider for his family. When their children were young, Darla innocently began to play Atari and Nintendo, then Sega. Over the years this "harmless" pastime used up many hours during the day and went late into the night. This activity led to playing online role-playing games. That is how Darla met a man online from another country. In fact, her role-playing character had an online marriage with his character. This man is younger than she, and their bond started as many online and person-to-person friendships do—very innocently.

Darla became more aloof. She was caught lying and began to pull away from many close friends. She was spending more and more time online chatting with this other man. My sister, a trusted friend of hers, received a call from Darla. She told my sister that in the past few months she had started feeling sorry for Nathan. He knew about this guy in another country, and Darla felt bad that he did not also have "someone to talk to." Darla's simple solution was to introduce her husband to a woman online.

Within weeks Nathan visited his new computer friend—a soon-to-be-divorced mother of two who lived just hours away. In less than two months Nathan and Darla decided to divorce. The other woman and her children moved into the house with Darla, Nathan, and their family. According to Darla, she's thankful her husband has "found someone," and they're reportedly happier than anyone could have imagined. This whole scenario is abhorrent. An obvious defrauding is taking place.

A few years ago Dr. Laura Schlessinger hosted an hour-long TV show titled "When Is an Affair an Affair?" This program dealt with committed married people who had emotional relationships with people other than their partners. Some of these led to physical relationships; others did not. Dr. Laura summarized her feelings on the matter:

> Anything that could lead to an affair also qualifies as part of the affair. . . . It should be clear to you that relationships outside of marriage, whether by use of the Internet or by some other means of spending time together, are improper and a form of adultery no matter what you want to call it.
>
> Intimacy is not just about physical encounters. When someone shares inner feelings, secrets, desires, flirts or flatters, or even places himself or herself in a compromising situation, you are being intimate. The final analysis: all forms of intimacy should be reserved for the marital relationship or else you are taking something away. Something that belongs to the spouse and giving it to someone else. That wasn't what the vows were about.
>
> The ultimate deterrent to all of this is a strong set of moral values, rules, and standards. These keep you from even taking the first step. Because, for sure if you don't take that first step, you won't be there to take that final fatal step.

Dr. Laura also conducted a Web poll that day. The question was: "Should an emotional but non-physical relationship be considered an affair?" The results back up the thesis of this book: 72 percent said yes; 28 percent said no.

We are all beginning to see the role of emotions. Darla formed an emotional connection with that young man. She defrauded him and vice versa. Do you see it? Satan saw the weakness and used it to his advantage. It's still hard for me to believe that a strong emotional attachment, the object of which is unseen, became the sole basis for Darla's willingness to throw away her marriage and family. It's been over a year since she met her online friend. Darla spent the holidays with this man—not even returning for Christmas. How sad!

Can emotions be trusted? Would you say Darla committed emotional defrauding? Would you call it adultery? For those who think that this emotional purity and defrauding stuff is a big joke, please rethink your position. Darla herself once held that opinion, telling my sister that she didn't understand why people would "save" themselves emotionally for marriage. Well, Satan used that lack of understanding in Darla to destroy friendships, trust, children's lives, a marriage, a family, and a relationship with God.

Emotional defrauding can pull any of us away from the Lord. All types of relationships—innocent friendships or even Darla and her e-mail buddy—can have devastating effects on one's marriage and children when people do not remain emotionally pure.

chapter SIXTEEN

Continuing My Journey

IN MY YEARS OF SHARING the message of emotional purity with countless men and women, I always get one question: How do you know whom to marry if you never open up emotionally?

Before I met my husband, my answer was all based on what I *thought* God could do. Even in my own private moments I wondered, *How will this really work itself out?* But now that I am married, I can look back and see what God had planned for me. My answer now is based on what God did with my faithfulness to Him.

Backtrack

In my early twenties I was ready to be married. So naturally when a nice, godly, good-looking Christian guy started to pay special attention to me, my mind started to think about marriage. Could he actually be the one for me? A flood of thoughts and feelings rushed through me, and I assumed that he felt the same way. Boy, was I wrong!

Many of you have been through a relationship that has left you hurt, confused, and brokenhearted. I've been there, and I know how it feels to be rejected, to have dreams and hopes discarded, leaving feelings of disorientation and confusion. I know the frustration of having unanswered questions. I know what it's like to have countless imaginary conversations of what you would say to him if you had the chance. I know what it's like to be Tracy. I can sympathize with many of you.

One relationship with a special guy friend looked like many of the ones you have probably experienced. We spent a lot of time together, just the two of us, sharing our dreams, hopes, and pains. We laughed together all the time. We had long conversations about the Bible, what God was teaching us, and how we were growing in our love for Him. We had our own private sayings and songs that would make us laugh.

However, in all the fun times I had with him, I was always left feeling that something was missing—the pieces were not all there, and the puzzle was never completed. Questions reigned in my thoughts, and confusion was my number one emotion. I knew that Satan is the father of lies (John 8:44), but I still tried to push those questions aside, listening to the lies and relishing the attention my friend was giving me.

Can you relate? Maybe it all hits home too closely. The wounds may be deep and even fresh. Some of you have perhaps never been in an undefined emotional relationship, but I bet that you have spent a lot of mental energy thinking about a guy—someone who never felt the way you did.

Once I realized that the relationship I had with my friend was going to be nothing more than a friendship, my own personal healing started to take place. God began to show me what emotional purity looked like and how He wanted this level of purity to be a part of my life. He also set me on the path of healing so I'd be ready for my husband when the time came.

Healing

God uses all things in our lives to work together for good (Rom. 8:28). Looking back, I know He used this relationship to heal not only my heart, but also the hearts of countless other women and men who have had the pain of a broken relationship.

I did several things in order to find healing from this relationship. First of all, I began journaling my thoughts. The more I wrote, the more I found healing in getting it all down on paper. I began to see how I had contributed to my own pain. I had let my mind run ahead of me. I had fantasized about guys, relationships, and the hope of a relationship. I created situations to be near a certain guy. Sure, he may have treated me as special, but it was still my responsibility to keep my thought life under the full submission of my Lord.

Along with my writing, I began to devour God's Word, and I found countless verses that healed, encouraged, and challenged me in this area. I wrote out many verses that helped me heal, including:

> Wait for the LORD;
> be strong, and let your heart take courage;
> wait for the LORD! (Ps. 27:14)

> You are my hiding place and my shield;
> I hope in your word. (Ps. 119:114)

> Do not be anxious about anything, but in everything by prayer and supplication with thanksgiving let your requests be made know to God. (Phil. 4:6)

I also wrote pages and pages of prayers to the Lord. Even now I am encouraged by what the Lord did in those times. Many days I'd spend hours reading the Word, fasting, and seeking Him. I fell in love with God. This was my biggest crush ever, and it was so satisfying!

Not only did I plunge into God's Word, I backed off from guys totally. I kept my emotions in check and allowed myself to be content in God alone. I needed to take a step back in order to see clearly what lay ahead. Looking back, I realize that as I worked to pull away from guys, the Lord put me in hiding.

I prayed that the Lord would make me aware of when I was getting ahead of His timing. On many occasions the Lord would tap me gently on the shoulder and say, "Heather, you're doing it again. Stay fixed on Me." It was such a beautiful season of my life—just the Lord and me.

I also gave up the notion of getting married. This was a miracle because in my own strength I never could have accomplished such a feat. I remember a girlfriend who came to visit. She had her entire wedding planned out. She knew what her colors were and where the ceremony would be and even had a wedding dress hanging in her closet. The problem was, she didn't even know when she was getting married! At that moment I realized I was not at the same place as her. God had granted me contentment with being single—I felt that deep in my heart. It's not that I didn't want to ever get married, but I was happy even if God chose to keep me single for the rest of my life. That freeing moment left me standing in awe at God's miraculous work in my life.

The final step in my healing process was to forgive the guy and to forgive myself. I'm not sure whether or not the guy knowingly led me on, but I needed to forgive him for how he'd hurt me. Forgiving him came over time. A few years away from the situation gave me the perspective I needed.

Forgiving myself was more difficult. It was easy to beat myself up and say, "If only I had done something differently, I could have avoided this whole situation." But the Lord works out everything for good for those who love Him. I needed to trust that promise.

With these steps in my own healing, I saw how God was preparing my heart afresh for my husband, John. Of course, God took six years to repair me and prepare me for what He had in store for John and me, but it was well worth the wait.

Have You Met John Patenaude?

The first time I saw John Patenaude he was playing Peter in the Zion Passion Play at Christ Community Church in 2000. When the Peter denial scene came, I looked at him and thought, *There's a nice-looking Christian guy who's married with two kids. I'm sure his wife is in the audience.* I have no idea why I thought this about him.

The next weekend was Easter, and I spent it with my mom's extended family. That day I started to hear about "Peter" (I found out his name was actually John) for the first time. In fact, the guy was sort of woven into the fabric of my extended family. My grandma and John's aunt grew up together, and my uncle and John's brother went to high school together. John's dad coached my uncle in basketball. My mom's cousin sang in choir with him. And most of my relatives saw John as their chiropractor. Although I did not know John, everyone in my extended family did.

From that Easter on, it seemed that everyone I came across who knew John would say to me, "Have you met John Patenaude? You two would be great together." It almost became predictable. Even a lady at my dad's office, who knew my dad had three single daughters, asked if we had ever met John Patenaude.

In 2001, with my great-aunt's encouragement, my sisters and I went up to Camp Zion (the camp John's church owns) as cooks. At camp we had a great time of fellowship with the other staff, all of whom went to Christ Community Church (CCC). When we were on our way home, we talked about how great it would be to change churches and attend CCC, but we were afraid other family members would think we wanted to go just to meet this single guy. When we got home, however, and started to share with our parents all that had happened, my dad told us what the Lord had laid on his heart during the week we were gone.

During that week my dad decided to seek employment at another company. He also decided to start attending CCC and wanted to move to Zion. The three of us were speechless. We couldn't believe what we were hearing. Within ten days we bought a new house and sold our old house and my dad started his new job. God was moving fast.

Just after John turned thirty on August 11, 2001, one of his patients told him he needed go to a new church where there were more single women. John nicely told the man that he didn't go to church to meet a wife but to worship. It's a good thing he did not take that person's untimely advice—not more than two weeks later our family (which included three single women) started to attend CCC.

Our first Sunday I waited in the lobby as my two sisters went to the bathroom. An older gentleman walked up to me and said, "I don't think I've met you. My name is Paul Patenaude." Yes, the first person I met at CCC was John's dad. I almost died right there. All I could think was, "Oh no! My family is going to think I headed right for John's dad!" I introduced myself and explained my relationship to the rest of the Paulsen family. He said, "Well, it's nice to meet you." I said the same thing and got away as fast as I could.

Since I had heard about John for over a year and a half, I thought for sure my aunts and uncles were badgering him about me. But I was wrong. The first Sunday we were there, John had seen our family and thought, *Hmm, a family with three daughters. They must be on vacation.* After a few weeks he realized we were not on vacation. It wasn't long before John started to hear, "Have you met Heather Paulsen? You two would be good together."

John and I didn't meet until a year later. We knew who each other were, but because of all the talk we tried to avoid each other at all costs. One time we literally ran into each other as we came around a corner at church. We greeted each other and quickly went our separate ways.

Two and a Half Years

We "officially" met each other in September 2002—two and a half years after I had first heard, "Have you met John Patenaude? You two would be great together."

During those two and a half years I was tested over and over. I learned many things about John that made me desire to know him better. As I observed John and watched him interact with others, I was able to gain a lot of information about his character, and I liked what I saw.

A lot had changed in my life since my days of writing in my journals about guys. I wanted to maintain emotional purity. I did not want to run ahead of my heart with John. Countless things about him made me feel he could be "the one." We had never spoken to each other, so I was careful to guard my heart. I had to declare war on my thoughts; so I set up a battle plan.

I had to keep my thought life under the control of the Lord. When I felt myself wanting to daydream about meeting John, I would ask the Lord to help me wait on His timing and His plan. I did not want to waste another moment of my mental energy on anyone other than my husband, and at that time I did not know if John would be my husband or not.

Again God's Word became a great resource. Verses such as "Delight yourself in the LORD, and he will give you the desires of your heart" (Ps. 37:4) and "Be still before the LORD and wait patiently for him" (Ps. 37:7a) became my constant companions. God's Word is *the* place to start when you are faced with any trial, struggle, or frustration.

My battle plan was tested weekly. John sang in the choir, and every Sunday, no matter where I sat, I could see him in the choir loft. I didn't dare look at him; so I began to study the large stained-glass window in our church. Few people know that there is only one orange square in the whole window . . .

I remember one Sunday really fighting in my heart to stay emotionally pure. I was so tempted to drift to La-la Land and think about him. I longed to know him and to be known by him, but I knew full well it wasn't the Lord's time. One Sunday during our prayer time at church, God reminded me of Abraham who was asked to sacrifice the one thing that meant so much to him—his son Isaac. God impressed upon my mind the vision of getting up on the altar myself and lying there with a blanket covering me. I knew He was asking me to be still and to fully give Him control. It became a very powerful image in my mind and stuck with me when I would continue to see John on Sundays.

I did not, however, always follow my own advice. Plenty of times I tried to find ways to meet John. Auditions and rehearsals for CCC's Passion Play were starting up again, and I thought to myself, *If I join the Passion Play cast, I'll get to meet John.* Wouldn't you know that in the sixty-three years the church has done the play, it has only been canceled one time (due to a fire). Yet that very year it had to be canceled for a second time because there were not enough cast members!

When I found out it was canceled, I just had to laugh. The Lord made sure I did not run ahead of His timing.

Again I turned to my journal and poured out my struggle:

April 21, 2001: Went to see the Passion Play [John was again in the play in 2001]. Two ships passing in the night. Have yet to meet! There is a great chasm. This is a test of the intimacy relationship police. I won't meet him until I do absolutely nothing, nothing to make it happen.

August 6, 2001: Last night I couldn't stop thinking about "the guy." [I never used his name.] I drive myself crazy and here I am trying to be emotionally pure. Well, it's still a battle.

September 10, 2001: He has NO reason to introduce himself to me. I long to find mental peace with this situation. I long to know the answer—yes or no. I want to scream I am so annoyed. The battle to keep myself fixed on what the Lord wants continues in full force.

November 25, 2001: I'm not looking for a friend—I am looking for or wanting a husband, so if he is not going to be my husband, then I don't want to know him.

It was not long after I wrote that last entry that I knew I needed to stop writing about John and focus on what the Lord had for me. I spent much of the next few months traveling and speaking.

As I read some of my entries, I laugh. The Lord knew what He was up to. I just had to wait for Him. You can also clearly see that I was in a battle.

I struggled in my mind and heart, yet the Lord was faithful. He knew my desire was to stay emotionally pure, and He covered me with His grace in order to persevere. There were also plenty of journal entries about what the Lord was doing in my life and how He was challenging me to keep on growing.

After We Met

Once John and I *finally* met, the Lord gave us plenty of opportunities to spend time together. We spent most of our time with John's family. John lived next door to his brother and sister-in-law, and I became friends with them. John and I hung out together all the time; so I easily got to know him better.

As our interest in each other grew, I knew I had to keep my motives in check. I did not want people thinking I used his family to get to know John. I also did not want to go over to his family's house unless I knew my motives were pure. I was not the only one who was longing to spend more time together, however. He told me after we began dating that he'd get home from work and look for my car. If he saw it, he'd find some excuse to come over and visit.

I enjoyed time with John, and during those months we spent time with my family, his family, and our friends. We came up with plenty of other excuses to spend time together and were even, finally, in the Passion Play together.

Years before I met John, I had prayed that from the day I met my husband until the day I knew we were going to be married would be six months. Six months after meeting John, it became evident that we needed to define our relationship. He was treating me differently, and my heart was ready to burst. I knew that if he was not interested in a relationship with me, I needed to back off totally.

So on March 11, 2003, after our Passion Play practice, we decided to get food from Taco Bell and go back to my house. Little did John know that I had planned to have the DTR (define the relationship) talk with him. I had rehearsed in my mind over and over what I wanted to say. I knew I had to say something.

We ate our tacos and made small talk. In those six months of getting to know each other, we had never had a serious talk. This was only the third time we had been alone with each other. I mustered up the courage to ask, "What's going on between us? You seem to treat me differently, and I was wondering what you think about our relationship. I kind of like you, but I'm not sure how you feel." I know I said some other unscripted things as my nerves took over.

He looked at me and said, "Well, I like you as well and would like to see what our friendship could become."

I told him that I only date to see if it could lead to marriage; he agreed. So I said, "What are we then?"

"I guess we're boyfriend and girlfriend," he said with a smile.

"Well, let's shake on it then," I said (I'm not joking). We proceeded to shake hands as if we were closing a business deal—to this day we laugh at ourselves. You have to remember, neither one of us had really ever dated before. We were clueless on the proper rules of dating.

After we made that commitment, we both felt the freedom to express ourselves to each other. We finally talked about meaningful things and enjoyed getting to know each other's hearts. We both felt protected by the commitment we had made.

Five days later we were planning our wedding. A few weeks later John proposed at the top of the John Hancock Center in downtown Chicago. A short three months later we were married.

The Benefits

Over and over in my book I have written about the benefits of saving yourself emotionally for a committed relationship. When I first wrote this book, I was single and John was not in the picture. Part of me wondered what all those benefits would look like. I wondered if, when I finally got married, my commitment to emotional purity would really make any difference. Once in a relationship with John, I began to see all the benefits of having saved ourselves emotionally for each other.

The most amazing benefit was the fact that John and I trusted each other from day one. We were never scared that we were going to pull the rug out from under each other. Just recently we were talking about how we were able to completely trust each other so early in our relationship. It was pure, undefiled, and entirely lovely.

We had unbridled enjoyment in our relationship because we trusted in God's provision and were fixed on what God was doing in our relationship. It was pure joy from the very beginning.

We also laid a solid foundation for our marriage. Since each of us had complete trust in the other, we were able to find great security and vulnerability together.

Within a week of our starting to date, we set up some rules for our relationship. I hesitate to use the word *rules*—they are more like promises to each other. One was that we would always be each other's number-one cheerleader. We'd have each other's back and be on each other's team. We would never criticize the other person to anyone, and we would encourage and challenge each other. These promises have drawn us closer to each other as the years have gone on.

Another promise we made was to always communicate our feelings honestly. John had never been in a relationship with anyone where he fully exposed his heart. Over the months of our courtship I learned about what he felt and thought and how he viewed the world. It was a wonderful journey to take with him. Even now John and I make a point to talk about whatever we are thinking, and this has led to an extremely satisfying aspect of our marriage. I am grateful to know I can bring anything to John consequence-free, and he will listen and process before jumping to conclusions or becoming upset.

Over the years that John and I have been married, we have yet to have a fight. Let me clarify. We have had a couple of what we like to call "agitation sessions" with each other. We have been annoyed or frustrated, but we have avoided full-blown fights. I am not sure if this is a direct benefit of remaining emotionally pure with each other, but with the openness, honesty, and trust we had from day one, we have always been able to talk about things before a fight breaks out.

Not only were John and I emotionally pure for each other—we were both virgins on our wedding day. Words cannot describe the extent to which we have both felt blessed by this fact. I know many people do not make it to their wedding day physically pure, but my prayer is that God's Word would pierce and convict many hearts to reach this goal. I also pray that God would restore and give peace to those who have regretted their actions in this area. Remember, enormous joy and peace come from following God's will.

Waiting

Each one of you will have to make the decision about how willing you are to wait for God to write your love story. Waiting for God is not always an easy task, but in the end His blessings will far outweigh any blessing you can imagine. He longs to bless His obedient children.

Now that I am a mom, I can understand more of the Lord's heart as a parent. I enjoy blessing my children with good things when they are obedient and when they wait for my timing. I long to give them good things, but I also know that when they are disobedient or selfish I need to weed that out of their hearts.

My prayer is that you will find hope in my testimony of what the Lord did in my life. He helped me to remain emotionally whole for John and blessed me for waiting. The core of emotional purity is waiting on God's perfect timing.

chapter SEVENTEEN

Enjoying Your Single Years

ENJOY YOUR YEARS AS A SINGLE. Befriend them. Ninety percent of people walk down the aisle at least once. Rejoice in God's allowing you to be single and to serve and enjoy Him distraction-free. Chances are, you will be married a lot longer than you will be single. Don't waste time twiddling your thumbs and wondering when you are going to take the plunge into marriage.

Guard your emotions, and protect your heart from making mistakes. Save yourself—emotionally, spiritually, and physically—for your mate. The rewards of doing so will long outlast any momentary dissatisfaction you may experience in your singleness.

Soak in all the information you can regarding what it means to be a godly man or woman. Seek the Lord with all your time, energy, money, and strength. He will not return anything void.

I believe most of you picked up this book because you were looking for a solution to your dating woes. Now you may be thinking, *Well, she did give me a new way to think about this dating thing, but I am not sure it is a commitment I want to make.* If you want to avoid pain in your dating relationships, you are going to have to make a change. You can't take the same path and expect a different outcome. You must take a totally new course.

My mom often says, "A man convinced against his will is of the same persuasion still." So this must come from your heart and from the Holy Spirit's convicting you. I pray that each of you, in your heart, will come to the place where God wants you.

Your new path is not always going to be easy or even fun, but we must have a renewing of our minds, hearts, and souls. If you are serious about your love relationship with the Lord, spend your single years falling in love with Him. He makes a perfect mate.

I heard a story of two angels. It is about the heart of our relationship with the all-powerful, all-knowing Father above. (I have done a little paraphrasing.)

One night two angels were staying at the home of a wealthy family. This family had almost everything they wanted—spare bedrooms, extra cars, and fine food. When the angels came to stay, the family did not give them a bedroom but put them in the basement. They did not want these angels to mess up any of their fine things.

In the middle of the night the older angel woke up the younger angel with his loud tools. He was repairing a hole in the wall of the basement. This perplexed the younger angel, but he was able to drift back to sleep.

The next night they went to the home of a poor couple. Their prize possession was a cow. This cow provided their meager income.

This sweet couple gave the two angels the only comfortable spot in the house to sleep, the hay bed, while they took the floor.

The next morning they all awoke to find that the cow had died in the middle of the night. This made the younger angel very upset. In a private moment he asked the older angel, "Why did you repair the hole in the wall of the rich folks and allow the cow to die?"

The older angel replied, "Behind that hole was a great deal of gold, and I did not want the rich couple to discover it. And in the middle of the night the angel of death came for the wife and I pleaded with him to take the cow."

Remember, God's way and timing will look far different than you imagine. He will do what is best for you, even if you struggle to understand.

Say this prayer with me:

Father, my life is in Your hands. You provide for me moment by moment. I ask that You open my eyes to see Your unfailing love for me and help my stubborn heart to trust You fully. I know that I will not be single a day longer than You want me to be, and in that I will find rest from this mind game of wondering and waiting. Open doors of ministry for me so that I may serve where You want me to serve. Help me protect my emotions from the pitfall of having intimacy before commitment. All I could want or all that could satisfy me is wrapped up in my relationship with You. Allow me to rest in You and to fall more in love with You each day. In Your Son's holy and precious name, Jesus, Amen.

Questions for Study and Discussion

Chapter 1: Tracy and Mike

1. Which character—Tracy, Mike, Emma, or Chrissy—did you most relate to and why?

2. Before Chrissy came into the picture, what was your impression of Tracy and Mike's friendship?

3. If you were writing Tracy and Mike's next phone conversation, what would they say?

4. How could setting up emotional boundaries have saved Tracy from the pain she felt at the end of the story?

5. What were some of the red flags that indicated that Tracy and Mike were becoming too emotionally intimate too quickly?

6. What creates an emotional attachment between two people?

7. How do you emotionally bond with those around you?

Chapter 2: Avoiding Early Intimacy

1. How would you define emotional intimacy?

2. How is the Lord using the model of Christ and the church to change your outlook on male/female relationships?

3. How does Ephesians 5:22-32 lay a foundation for a God-honoring marriage?

4. How important is it for you to follow the example of Christ and the church in your marriage, even in your dating? Explain.

5. How can we discern if a relationship is moving past "friends"?

6. How would your relationship with a guy friend look if you considered him your brother in Christ?

7. What is the relationship between physical and emotional intimacy?

Chapter 3: Finding Good Guidance

1. What are the benefits of being emotionally pure in your opposite-sex relationships?

2. How might an older mentor provide wise advice on your path toward marriage?

3. What helps you obtain and maintain emotional purity? What hinders it?

4. How are generations separated or mixed in your church and social circles?

5. Who in your life could help you stay on the path of emotional purity?

Chapter 4: Guarding Your Heart

1. How should a man care for the heart of a woman?

2. In your own words, define emotional defrauding.

3. How does defrauding manifest itself in other areas of your life?

4. What are some ways you can prevent emotionally defrauding someone?

5. Why is an emotional but nonphysical relationship with a married person still an affair?

6. How would you treat your single friends differently if you saw them as someone else's future mates?

7. How does someone care for the heart of a woman to ensure she is guarded from being devoted to the wrong guy?

8. What are some of the benefits of marrying your first love?

Chapter 5: Defining a Friendship

1. What are your thoughts on male/female friendships?

2. What does "just friends" mean?

3. How would you describe friendship with a godly brother/sister in Christ?

4. When did you cross into a deep emotional bond with someone?

5. Examine your current opposite-sex friendships. How do they line up with God's Word?

6. Why is it important to define relationships?

7. How can you keep your thoughts under control?

Chapter 6: Protecting Your Relationships

1. When have you given away your heart without a commitment? How did you feel?

2. What does commitment look like for you?

3. How would commitment before intimacy aid in remaining emotionally pure?

4. What are some benefits of having commitment before intimacy?

5. What level of devotion should a husband and wife have toward each other?

6. What could be your plumb line if you are questioning your actions toward a brother in the Lord?

Chapter 7: Learning True Contentment

1. When in your life has the sin of envy become all-consuming?

2. What things in your life would be classified as idols?

3. "Love the Lord your God with all . . . your mind" (Matthew 22:37). How is your thought life?

4. How does your attitude about being single change when you believe in God's sovereignty?

5. What does it mean to be content in Christ?

6. In what areas in your life are you not content?

7. How can you trust God during your single years?

Chapter 8: Trusting in God

1. What creates the idea that marriage will save us from singleness?

2. What's stopping you from fully trusting God to provide for all your needs?

3. Why does singleness scare some people?

4. What verses in the Bible speak about God's direction for our lives? Include some not mentioned in this chapter.

5. How can a lack of trusting God about your singleness put a wall between Him and you?

Chapter 9: Creating Safe Ideals

1. How has the "marriage is the prize of life" attitude affected you?
2. What are your expectations going into marriage?
3. How would you describe your prize of life?
4. What do you feel you need to know about your future spouse? In what ways can you learn these things without being emotionally intimate?

Chapter 10: Watching Your Feelings

1. How do you keep your sometimes unruly surface feelings lined up with the core of who God made you to be?
2. When have you pretended to be someone else in order to attract someone?
3. Think of a time in your life when you tried to satisfy a feeling or emotion outside of God's timing. What happened?
4. In what situations do you find yourself unable to control your feelings?
5. What is the difference between foundational and surface feelings?
6. How can you keep from feeding into your friends' complaints about singleness?
7. What is your purpose in being single?
8. Why do we rely on surface feelings to dictate our emotions?

Chapter 11: Understanding Your Expectations

1. What unmet expectations frustrate you?
2. When in your life did an unmet expectation take over?
3. What do you do when your expectations are unmet?
4. What do you do when your thoughts are not God-honoring or are self-focused?
5. How can you become friends with your expectations?
6. How can you "take every thought captive to obey Christ"?
7. How do we look to marriage to save us?

8. How can we keep from encouraging our friends' make-believe thoughts?
9. What is your battle plan to keep your thoughts captive?

Chapter 12: Following God's Plan

1. What does it look like when you focus your attention on your relationship with God?
2. What are some ways you can practice being selfless for your marriage?
3. How would finding joy in your singleness change the way you live now?
4. What activities do you need to be released from that do not foster a love relationship with Christ?
5. How does a single person focusing on self look different from a single person who is focusing on God?

Chapter 13: Seeing Christ's Design

1. How does marriage mirror a relationship with God?
2. What picture do you want to paint with your marriage? Why?
3. How do you feel about a man being the initiator?
4. Why is it important to have a marriage that points people to God?
5. How does your faith in God as your Savior relate to marriage?

Chapter 14: Preparing for Marriage

1. How would taking a step away from an unidentified emotional relationship help with your spiritual life?
2. What are ways you can get out of an unidentified emotional relationship?
3. How do you deal with your relationship baggage?
4. What type of training do you need in the "Wife Training Program"?
5. What would you add to that training program?
6. What does it mean for a wife to submit to her husband?
7. What does it mean to be submissive and have a gentle and quiet spirit?

Chapter 15: Dating Done Differently

1. How is this concept of dating different from your idea of dating?
2. How would this dating alternative benefit you?
3. What is God saying to you regarding your dating life?
4. What are ways you might protect yourself from becoming emotionally intimate with someone?

To contact the author regarding questions or speaking engagements, visit her blog:

www.emotionalpurity.blogspot.com